A FELLOW OF INFINITE JEST

By Thomas Yoseloff

THE MERRY ADVENTURES OF TILL EULENSPIEGEL
(co-author of children's version), 1944

SEVEN POETS IN SEARCH OF AN ANSWER
(editor), 1944

A FELLOW OF INFINITE JEST

By THOMAS YOSELOFF

New York PRENTICE-HALL, INC. *1945*

Printed in the United States of America

For Sara

For Sara

Contents

CONTENTS

AUTHOR'S NOTE

Sterne without recourse to that excellent work by Prof.
W. L. Cross, The Life and Times of Laurence Sterne. But
there have been few attempts to go behind the mass

Author's Note

JAMES BRANCH CABELL once bemoaned the fact
that it is the fate of "immortal" authors eventually to find
their destiny between the covers of high school "literature" anthologies. It is sad, however true, that the great
writers of the past are known to the American public
largely through high school and college textbooks, and
fame thus varies directly with the extent to which their
writings are considered proper reading for adolescents. It
follows then that a man's measure is taken by the most
innocuous and unsophisticated of his works; Defoe is
known only as the author of *Robinson Crusoe,* and not
one American in a hundred is aware that he also wrote a
book called *Moll Flanders; Gulliver's Travels* is the touchstone of Swift's career, while his superior works languish
on the shelves of scholars' libraries.

It is unfortunate for Sterne's memory that his writings
were designed largely for the consumption of intelligent
adults. You will look in vain through the high school anthologies for selections from Sterne. So, although Sterne's
literary influence transcended his own land, his own
time and even his own language, to shape the pattern of
current writing, to the great majority of American readers he remains practically unknown.

This is not written solely by way of criticism, but rather

by way of explanation. It is one clue in the mystery of
Sterne's neglect in this country; it goes hand in hand with
the fact that Sterne has received less of the attention he
deserves in the United States than in any other major
country on earth. There are several scholarly works available for students: no one could undertake a study of
Sterne without recourse to that excellent work by Prof.
W. L. Cross, *The Life and Times of Laurence Sterne*. But
there have been few attempts to go behind the mass of
scholarly research, letters and contemporary comment, to
find Sterne the man and present him, as he lived and
worked, in a book for the general reader.

"They order this matter better"—as Sterne would have
written it—elsewhere. In continental Europe, his influence
and importance made themselves more strongly felt and
have better endured. Sterne's work was translated into
French, German, and Italian, and gained thousands of dev-
otees in those countries. The practically insurmountable
difficulties in the translation of Sterne's language idiosyn-
crasies stood in the way of *Tristram Shandy,* but there
were fewer such difficulties in *A Sentimental Journey* (if
one excepts the word *sentimental* itself) and this book became a universal favorite for the ages almost immediately
after its publication. In Germany, especially, was the full
impact of Sterne's work upon the intellect and feeling
realized. Upon hearing of Sterne's death, Lessing is said
to have exclaimed, "I would have given ten years of my
own life, if I had been able to lengthen Sterne's by one
year." Goethe's praise was heartfelt, and how much the
Romantic school in Germany owed to Sterne is indicated
in Heine's estimate that Sterne was "the born equal of
William Shakespeare." We can not be sure whether the
Nazi official book burners got around to Sterne, but we
know that his influence remained in pre-Hitler Germany

to our own time, and no doubt remains today wherever German culture has survived the barbaric onslaught.

In what respects is our own country in our own age a debtor to Laurence Sterne? Today the literature of formal descriptive prose has been relegated to a secondary position, while our authors of first rank have deserted formality for the wider field of impressionism. Current literature is a literature of thoughts, feelings, desires and impulses. Its developments are stated not in terms of exterior view, but in terms of interior sensation. Sterne may justifiably be called the founder of this impressionistic school. The terse Anglo-Saxon realism of our time is actually blood-brother to Sterne's delightfully personal wanderings and digressions. He substituted for the stiff, heavily laden prose of his time an intimate conversational method. He defied the accepted rules of literary composition and wrote as he talked. Putting himself on the written page, he let his readers into his thoughts and beliefs, carried them along with him in his mental digressions, made them party to his own sensations. In this he is stylistic godfather to such a widely diverse group as James Joyce, Ernest Hemingway, Gertrude Stein, Sherwood Anderson, John Dos Passos and William Saroyan. In other ages, his influence has been felt in other ways, but today the stamp of his impressionism is clearly imprinted. Surely ours is an age which owes Sterne much and has paid him little.

This volume is the outgrowth of a study which began several years ago. It is entirely biographical; every detail is as accurate as wide reading and careful attention could make it. However, the aim has been to make this an interesting story for the casual reader; it is an effort to re-create the man as he was known to the contemporary world, to his intimates and to himself. I began this study prejudiced only by an admiration for Sterne's writings; I ended it with a respect for the man.

Rather than burden this work with footnotes and references throughout the text, I thought it desirable to list in this note some of the sources to which I referred in my study. Wherever material is quoted in the following pages, it will be duly credited. This is not intended to be a complete list of sources, but these works I found particularly valuable:

The writings of Sterne: *The Life and Opinions of Tristram Shandy, Gentleman,* nine volumes, in various editions; *A Sentimental Journey through France and Italy,* two volumes, in various editions; *The Sermons of Mr. Yorick,* seven volumes, in various editions; *The History of a Good Warm Watchcoat;* Sterne's autobiographical account, written for his daughter; the *Journal to Eliza;* other short works; and letters, in various editions.

The Life of Laurence Sterne, by Percy Fitzgerald; in two volumes; London, 1896.

The study on Sterne in *English Humorists,* by W. M. Thackeray, in various editions.

Sterne, by H. D. Traill, in *English Men of Letters* series, edited by John Morley; New York, 1901.

Sterne, a Study, by Walter Sichel; London, 1910.

The Life and Times of Laurence Sterne, by Wilbur L. Cross; in two volumes; New Haven, 1925.

The Letters of Laurence Sterne, with an introduction by R. Brimley Johnson; London, 1927.

Laurence Sterne in Germany, by H. W. Thayer; New York, 1905.

Garrick and His Circle, by Mrs. Clement Parsons; New York, 1906.

The Letters of Horace Walpole, edited by Mrs. Paget Toynbee; in eight volumes; Oxford, 1903.

I

The Jester at Court

IN THE London newspapers dated March 22, 1768, appeared the following brief announcement:

> Died at his lodgings in Bond Street, the Rev. Mr.
> Sterne. Alas poor Yorick! I knew him well; a fellow
> of infinite jest, most excellent fancy, &c.
> Wit, humor, genius, hadst thou, all agree;
> One grain of wisdom had been worth the three!

So in death all London eulogized and damned Sterne in the character in which it had known him during the last eight years of his life—the character of Yorick, the king's jester. Fashionable London had been his court. The homes of the wealthy and the noble were opened to him, and on his annual visits to the city his engagement book was filled with dinners and receptions for weeks in advance. In an age when the ability to turn a good quip—preferably a risqué one—was considered a high mark of character, London welcomed Sterne as the playboy cleric, the naughty wit whose epigrams might be repeated for weeks over dinner tables and in fashionable salons. Like the king's fool in cap and bells, whose name he took, Sterne jested for his supper, paid with brilliant quips for his welcome into London society.

His fame as a wit spread through England and the Continent, and even to America. Traveling through France when relations between that country and England were strained, he was able to secure a passport without difficulty:

> ——*A man who laughs,* said the duke, *will never be dangerous.*——Had it been for anyone but the king's jester, added the Count, I could not have gotten it these two hours.——*Pardonnez moi,* Mons. le Count, said I——I am not the king's jester.——But you are Yorick?——Yes.——*Et vous plaisantez?*——I answered, Indeed I did jest——but was not paid for it——'twas entirely at my own expence.
>
> We have no jester at court, Mons. le Count, said I; the last we had was in the licentious reign of Charles II.——since which time our manners have been so gradually refining, that our court at present is so full of patriots, who wish for *nothing* but the honours and wealth of their country——and our ladies are all so chaste, so spotless, so good, so devout——there is nothing for a jester to make a jest of——
>
> *Voila un persiflage!* cried the count.

So even in denying his character as the court jester, Sterne was able to turn the explanation to his advantage with a jest.

If the character in which most of London knew Sterne represented the whole story, a picture of the man would come to us easily. But while he was coining a quip, he was writing tender, devoted letters to the daughter for whom he had a deep and unswerving love; he was preparing for whatever financial sacrifices might be necessary to insure the comfort of a nagging wife from whom he had been long estranged; he was losing his heart and head in a love affair which went with him to the grave; and he was creating a family of living portraits which keep Sterne's fame alive long after his jests have lost much of their meaning and his style has lost the attraction of novelty.

The very contradictions that complicate Sterne's character help to explain the man to us. Thackeray, who owed much to Sterne, despised him for his weaknesses; Byron turned to advantage a phrase on Sterne's hypocrisy; another denounced him for his plagiarisms; a fourth for his cowardice; a fifth for his profligacy. His defenders have shielded him from one charge or another, often half-heartedly. Many in that scholarly procession of Sterne's commentators stand now like the three blind men who grasped the elephant's tail, trunk and tusk, and declared the elephant to be like a rope, a tree and a stone. Each of his detractors and defenders has felt a segment of Sterne's life or character and tried to build a whole man out of the part. Yet it must be clear that a man's life is not expressed in a phase, a moment or a mood. It is a combination of moods, thoughts, feelings and actions, subtly interwoven, that determine a man's final stature, and it is impossible to see the pattern by grasping a few loose threads.

It was in 1760 that London first heard of Laurence Sterne. There had been published and placed on sale in York two slim volumes, the first of *The Life and Opinions of Tristram Shandy, Gentleman*. On the first day of January the London newspapers carried an announcement of publication, offering the books for sale. The name of the author was omitted; nor was any mention made of the nature of the books. But if Tristram Shandy came "still-born" into the world, at least he was attended by an excellent midwife. David Garrick was then at the height of his career in the London theatre and arbiter of fashionable taste. Copies of the volumes came to him, highly recommended by a friend. Garrick read and approved; by the time Sterne came to London in March the success of the volumes was assured.

It was on March 6 that Sterne came to call on Garrick, beginning a friendship that lasted the remainder of Sterne's life. Garrick introduced him into London society, and the visit that Sterne had expected would last a few weeks stretched out into nearly three months. His two slim volumes had created a stir in London such as he could never have believed possible in his most hopeful imaginings. By the time he had arrived in London the entire first edition was exhausted. Dodsley, the leading publisher, who had refused to incur the original expense of publishing the books, declaring them to be unsalable, bought the copyright for a figure which must have seemed a minor fortune to the poor clergyman. Within a week after his arrival in London, a second edition was announced.

Following Garrick's example, the nobility and the people of fashion read *Tristram Shandy*. Like its author, it went everywhere. Those who could not bring themselves to read and discuss it in the drawing room, read and discussed it in their bed-chambers. Within a few days after Sterne's arrival in London, the great houses of the town were opened to him, and the leaders of fashion were vying for the privilege of entertaining him. On March 8, only two days after his first meeting with Garrick, Sterne was writing to his York friend, Catherine de Fourmantelle:

> I have the greatest honors paid and most civilities shewn me that were ever known from the Great; and am engaged all ready to ten Noble Men and Men of fashion to dine. Mr. Garrick pays me all and more honour than I could look for. I dined with him today, and he has promised Numbers of great People to carry me to dine with 'em. He has given me an order for the Liberty of his Boxes, and of every part

of his House for the whole Season; and indeed leaves
nothing undone that can do me either Service or
Credit——

Sterne was in his forty-seventh year when he burst like
a meteor over London. For years he had worked, an obscure clergyman in an unimportant parish, in straitened
financial circumstances, denied preferment in the church.
Suddenly, almost by accident it seemed, there opened before him a new and brilliant vista, in which wealth, position and preferment came without effort. In place of the
unpleasantness which had been his share through all the
years of his life, a pleasant road lay ahead. And all that
was necessary to travel it was the jester's cap and bells.
It is little wonder indeed that Sterne's head was turned by
his London success.

London cared little for the many fine qualities of *Tristram Shandy,* which have made it immortal—the portraits
of Walter Shandy, my uncle Toby, and Trim; the keen
satire leveled against scholastic erudition. London took
the Shandys to its heart for the sake of the risqué character
of the books, the double-entendre anecdotes, the bizarre
style of Sterne's composition.

London welcomed Laurence Sterne as Yorick, the court
jester, and upon Yorick it showered its largess. Laurence
Sterne tried on the cap and the jester's costume and found
them not uncomfortable. And in the remaining eight
years of his life he seldom took them off in public.

a meteor over London. Fifteen years he had worked, an obscure clergyman in an unimportant parish, in snatched

II

Shandean Beginnings

As THOUGH a perverse providence were determined
to give Laurence Sterne's entrance into the world a true
Shandean flavor, it selected the worst possible moment for
his birth. It was in November, 1713; the Peace of Utrecht
had provided a breathing spell for war-torn Europe, and
the British regiments which had remained in Flanders
after the signing of the treaty were returning to England.
One of the last of the regiments to return was the 34th
regiment of foot, and among the returning soldiers was a
young ensign, Roger Sterne, then not more than twenty-
one years old. The troops were brought from Dunkirk
to Clonmel, in the south of Ireland, and the day after
their arrival the regiment was disbanded and the men
were left to shift for themselves.

Young Sterne was already burdened with a wife and
child, and at this untimely moment a second put in his
appearance. Thus Ireland became by force of circumstance the birthplace of Laurence Sterne. On the twenty-
fourth of November, 1713, he began a nomadic existence
which made him for the first decade of his life an unwit-
ting follower of the fortunes of war.

Sterne traced his descent from an old Suffolk family,
one branch of which had been established in Nottingham-

shire. The first of the family to bring fame to the name was Dr. Richard Sterne, Archbishop of York, who had a long and distinguished career as a churchman and as a Master of Jesus College, Cambridge. A serious, conservative scholar whose remarkable feat of research was a thesis on the *3600 faults in our printed Bibles,* Dr. Sterne was an enthusiastic supporter of the Stuarts. During the brief republic of Oliver Cromwell he fell out of favor and was subjected to numerous indignities, but upon the restoration of the royalty he was made Archbishop of York, where he remained for twenty years, until his death in 1683. Among the Archbishop's benefactions were six scholarships which he established at Cambridge, and which, a half century later, made possible the education of his great-grandson Laurence. Had the scholarly ecclesiast been able to foresee *Tristram Shandy,* he might have repented of his liberality!

Dr. Sterne married one Elizabeth Dickinson, and to the couple were born thirteen children, the third of whom was Simon Sterne of Halifax. To the eight hundred pounds in moneys and East India stock which he received as his share of the Archbishop's estate, Simon Sterne was able to add the fortune of Mary Jaques, heiress to the lordship of Elvington. Out of his marriage with the wealthy heiress were born three sons and three daughters.

The eldest son, Richard, fell heir to the estates of his father, married well and amassed a fortune. It was he who aided Laurence later in his education. The youngest son, Jaques, entered the Church and also exerted an influence—albeit a bitter one—on Laurence's career.

But it is the second son, Roger, the young ensign of Chudleigh's regiment, with whom we are mostly concerned. Of a restless disposition, he was enticed neither by the prospect of a good marriage nor by a career in the church. The only career open to him which fitted his mood was a life in the army. In 1708 he enlisted, and the next year he was sent to the Netherlands, where his regiment served in garrison duty for several months. In 1710 the regiment joined Marlborough's army and served until the conclusion of the Peace of Utrecht.

"My father," Laurence Sterne wrote in the memoir to his daughter, "was a little smart man active to the last degree in all exercises, most patient of fatigue and disappointments, of which it pleased God to give him full measure. He was, in his temper, somewhat rapid and hasty, but of a kindly, sweet disposition, void of all design; suspected no one; so that you might have cheated him ten times in a day, if nine had not been sufficient for your purpose."

Nevertheless, he was probably improvident by nature, as well as restless and hasty tempered, and he incurred the displeasure of his family by an ill-advised marriage when he was only nineteen years old. Finding himself in debt to one Nuttle, a sutler in Flanders during Queen Anne's war, Roger settled the score by marrying Nuttle's stepdaughter, Agnes Hebert, a woman already widowed and probably some years the young ensign's senior.

Now began a life of travels that is pathetic in the recital. Roger's wife was a prolific woman; hardly a year passed without adding a new burden to the young soldier's difficulties. The children shared the hardships and dangers of the barracks, with its uncertain existence and its wanderings, and few of them survived an infancy so spent. Roger Sterne's babies, as Laurence wrote later, were "not made to last long."

The first child born to the couple was a girl, named Mary, who came into the world on July 10, 1712, in French Flanders. She had her first experience as a trav-

eler when she was only a year old, the regiment embarking at Dunkirk for Clonmel, where Laurence was born.
As soon as the baby could be carried, the family left Ireland and went to Elvington, the estate of Simon Sterne,
where his widow Mary Jaques was living. The wayward
son and his family were given asylum here and remained
for about ten months, when the regiment was again banded
together and ordered to Dublin.

So again the babies were bundled up and taken across
the narrow channel to Ireland. However, within a month
the young soldier was ordered to Exeter, and he left his
family behind in Dublin, to follow him later, "in a sad
winter." Sterne, writing to his daughter years later, called
it a "melancholy" journey, and melancholy it must surely
have been. We can imagine the harassed and tired
mother, with two children to care for and pregnant with
a third, embarking in the cold of winter on a draughty
vessel for Liverpool, and traveling by uncertain stages
overland to Plymouth.

At Plymouth the third child, Joram, was born, choosing
a moment hardly more opportune than that of Laurence's
birth to put in his appearance. The young mother joined
her husband, but before a year had passed he was ordered
back to Dublin, and the whole family embarked again for
Ireland. The memoir relates a narrow escape from death
for the whole family when the vessel sprang a leak. But
the pathetic little band survived and after many difficulties
arrived again in Dublin.

Evidently in the hope of establishing a permanent home
for his family, the young ensign took a large house and
furnished it, spending "a great deal of money." But this
domestic venture was to prove as unstable as the rest of
the ensign's projects. In 1719, when Laurence was five
years old, "all unhinged again; the regiment was ordered,

with many others, to the Isle of Wight, in order to embark
for Spain in the Vigo expedition." Again the long journey, by sea and by land, to the Isle of Wight, a journey
which was made sad by the death of little Joram.

While the regiment went abroad on the Vigo expedition, the mother and her two children remained on the
Isle of Wight. Shortly after their arrival, in September,
1719, another child, Anne, was born. When the regiment
returned to Ireland from its campaign abroad, Roger
Sterne again sent for his family to join him. His wife,
with her three children, embarked for Ireland, but a
violent storm arose and the ship was forced to put back to
Wales, where the family remained for a month. At last
they were able to cross the water and they rejoined the
ensign in the barracks at Wicklow long after he had given
up hope of ever again seeing them alive.

In the course of a year's residence in the barracks at
Wicklow, another son, Devijeher, was born. About seven
miles from Wicklow was the parsonage of a Mr. Fether-
ston, a relative of Mrs. Sterne, and the mother brought
her four children to the parsonage to stay for several
months. One incident of his life in the parsonage at
Animo Sterne recalled vividly enough to record in his
memoir more than forty years later.

> It was in this parish, during our stay, that I had the
> wonderful escape in falling through a mill-race whilst
> the mill was going, and of being taken up unhurt.
> The story is incredible, but known for truth in all
> that part of Ireland, where hundreds of the common
> people flocked to see me.

The story is made doubly incredible by a coincidence
almost too unusual to be true. It was told by his great-
grandfather, the Archbishop, that such an accident occurred to him when he was a child. Playing near a mill-

race, he fell into the sluice and would have been crushed to death by the water-wheel, had not one bucket in the wheel been missing—the one which providence chose to bring down at that instant.   However, it is not beyond the realm of possibility that the same accident might have befallen both the Archbishop and his great-grandson, and we can accept the story as a memorable incident in Sterne's early life.   The picture of the natives coming from miles around to see the child who had had such a miraculous deliverance is an interesting sidelight on the life of the Irish villages.

The months at the parsonage were soon past, and the family again went to Dublin to take up a year's existence in the barracks.   Here Sterne records two important events—his learning to write and the death of "a pretty blossom," his sister Anne.   Sterne continues the memoir from this point:

> The regiment ordered to Carrickfergus, in the north of Ireland.   We all decamped, but got no further than Drogheda;—thence ordered to Mullengar, forty miles west, where, by Providence, we stumbled upon a kind relation, a collateral descendant from Archbishop Sterne, who took us all to his castle and kindly entertained us for a year, and sent us to the regiment at Carrickfergus, loaded with kindnesses, &c.   A most rueful and tedious journey had we all (in March) to Carrickfergus, where we arrived in six or seven days.—Little Devijeher here died; he was three years old: . . . . another child sent to fill his place, Susan.   This babe too left us behind in this weary journey.

Thus, out of the seven children born to Roger Sterne and his wife, only three, Laurence, Mary, and Catherine (born after Laurence had gone away to school) survived. Mary was "the most unfortunate."   She married a shiftless spendthrift in Dublin, who left her to die in poverty and despair. Catherine's story will enter our narrative later. As for Roger Sterne, the misfortunes that had harried him through his life continued to the end. Having been sent with his regiment to Gibraltar, he quarreled with Captain Christopher Phillips over a goose. In the duel which followed he was run through the body with a sword, and although he survived, he had lost the strength for his rigorous career. He was sent to Jamaica, where he fell ill of a fever peculiar to the country at the time, "which took away his senses first, and made a child of him, and then, in a month or two, walking about continually without complaining, till the moment he sat down in an arm chair and breathed his last—which was at Port Antonio, on the north of the island."

By the time he was eleven years old, Laurence was considered ready for school. A minor controversy has arisen over the name of the grammar school in which the young pupil was "fixed." His memoir reports very briefly, "My father got leave of his colonel to fix me at school—which he did near Halifax, with an able master." There were at that time two schools located near Halifax—one at Heath and the other at Hipperholme. Sterne's early biographers accepted the old tradition that he had studied at Heath, but later evidence seems to point to Hipperholme as the more likely of the two. Until more conclusive evidence is available, the identity of the "able master" who gave the first impetus to *Tristram Shandy* must remain uncertain.

While he was in the grammar school he was under the care of his uncle Richard Sterne, heir to the Elvington estate. The boy, in common with the young students of the time, devoted his study to Latin, Greek and classical literature.

He was at best an indifferent student, and an old textbook which came into Percy Fitzgerald's hands nearly a

century and a half after Sterne used it indicates that the
boy spent more time sketching on its well-worn pages than
in reading it. As the biographer described it:

> It was a soiled, dirty book, every page scrawled over
> with writing, sketches, repetitions of his own name
> and those of his fellows—"L. S., 1728," the letters
> being sometimes twisted together in the shape of a
> monogram. On the title-page, in faint brown char-
> acters, was written, in straggling fashion, the owner's
> name: "Law: Sterne, September ye 6, 1725." We find
> also some of his schoolfellows' names. . . . There is
> a stave of notes, with the "sol fa," etc., written below,
> and signed "L. S." Then we come on this: "I owe
> Samuel Thorpe one halfpenny, but I will pay him
> today." On another page we read "labour takes
> panes". . . . But on nearly every page of this dog-
> eared volume was some rude drawing or sketch done
> after the favourite schoolboy rules of art. One curi-
> ous, long-nosed, long-chinned face has written over
> it, "This is Lorence," and there is certainly a coarse
> suggestion of the later chin and nose of the humour-
> ist. There are owls, and cocks and hens, etc., a pic-
> ture of "A gentleman," and several, as we might ex-
> pect, of soldiers. . . .

To sum it all up briefly, he was probably a typical
schoolboy. The race of schoolboys has changed but little
from the time when Shakespeare's young scholar crept,
"like snail unwillingly to school," to our own time. Certainly there is no justification here for Thackeray's denunciation of the boy as a leering, lying young reprobate.
In fact, one anecdote which Sterne himself gave to the
world in his memoir would seem to indicate the high regard which the "able master" had for his pupil.

The ceiling of the schoolroom had just been white-
washed, and the ladder used in the work was still standing
in the room. Young Laurence mounted the ladder and

wrote in heavy black letters with a brush, LAU. STERNE, across the newly painted ceiling. The usher of the school, discovering Sterne's artistic digression, took the boy in hand and administered a sound thrashing. "My master was very much hurt at this, and said before me," Sterne recalled some forty years later, "that never should that name be effaced, for I was a boy of genius, and he was sure I would come to preferment." (Perhaps this incident explains why Sterne recalled the man long after as an "able master.")

It was here that Sterne was initiated into the wonders of the world of books. If we accept portions of *Tristram Shandy* as autobiographical, the boy lived intensely in the books he was reading, showing early that capacity for feeling which characterized his writings. When he read the story of the siege of Troy, he was "as much concerned for the destruction of the Greeks and Trojans as any boy of the whole school." He suffered three strokes of the ferule, "for calling Helena a bitch for it." He wept over the death of Hector, and when Priam came to beg the dead youth's body, young Laurence was so affected that he could not eat his dinner.

We get from these fragments a picture of the boy during these years. He was tall, lank, indolent—but not more indolent than the schoolboy's ancient prerogative allows. He was already showing signs of that sensitiveness to the world that is so apparent in *Tristram Shandy* and even more so in the *Sentimental Journey;* and a sense of humor —sly and at times almost malicious—that was characteristic of the man in his last years was already visible. Certainly the painting on a freshly coated ceiling was malicious enough as a jest; yet its net effect was harmless, and at any rate it hardly justifies the symbolism found in it by a biographer, H. D. Traill, some years ago:

In itself, however, the urchin's freak was only too
unhappily characteristic of the man. The trick of be-
fouling what was clean (and because it was clean)
clung to him most tenaciously all his days; and many
a fair white surface—of humour, of fancy, or of sentiment—was to be disfigured by him in after years. . . .

Granted that portions of Sterne's writings are tinged with
indelicacy, we must nevertheless face the obvious fact that
many of the most delightful passages in his books owe
much to his "disfiguring" sense of humor. Rabelais with
the mental processes and style of Milton would not be
Rabelais.

Sterne spent some seven or eight years in the grammar
school near Halifax, and by 1731 he was ready for the
university. In the course of his last months as a pupil
came the word of his father's death, and the report must
have shocked the youth deeply. There is no doubt that
he loved his father, that "little smart man . . . . patient of
all fatigue and disappointments," whom he remembered
so kindly in later years.

Coming as it did in the last weeks of his years in the
grammar school, the death of his father is a line of demar-
cation in Sterne's life. With it ended his boyhood, and
he embarked on a more serious phase of his life: the university and preparation for service in the church. In his
earliest years had been sown the seeds of a nomadic restlessness, a discontent that found fruition in the wanderings of his last years. Out of his boyhood came bitter
memories of the rugged life of the army camps, which
found expression in *Tristram Shandy*. Those melancholy
journeys, the hard life of his boyhood, the sadness of a
sensitive boy at the death of his brothers and sisters, and
finally, the horrible death of his father—all left their mark
on the boy, and found expression later in his writings.

But equally important, from our point of view, he brought with him out of boyhood the beginnings of an omnivorous appetite for books, an appetite quickened by his friendship in the university with John Hall-Stevenson. The wide range of his appetite led him from Ovid and Homer to the military theorists of the seventeenth and eighteenth centuries, from Burton's *Anatomy of Melancholy* to Rabelais.   Under Hall-Stevenson's tutelage it found its way to the curious and bizarre, the delightful and little known which are the reward of the patient bibliophile.   And at last it gave to the world that compendium of erudition and satire, the paradox that is *Tristram Shandy*.

III

"Cousin Anthony"

STERNE, having begun his formal education at the comparatively late age of eleven, was eighteen before he was ready for the university. But even then there was a delay, so that it was not until he was twenty that he was admitted to Cambridge.

It is probable that the death of his father had proved a blow to Mrs. Sterne and her family. We find no further mention here of Mary, the eldest daughter, who must by this time have married the scoundrel Weemans whom Sterne mentions in his memoir. Laurence had been in his uncle's care for several years, so that Mrs. Sterne was left with the necessity of caring only for her youngest child, Catherine. After a visit to England with her daughter, she returned to Dublin, where she was able to live with the assurance of a pension of twenty pounds annually. While this was hardly enough to provide mother and daughter with luxuries, it was sufficient for the necessities of an ordinary existence.

Laurence was left again in his uncle's care, his mother being unable to contribute anything to the boy's support. However, in 1732, his uncle, who had been in ill health, died suddenly, and Laurence was again left at the mercies of the world. His uncle's estates at Elvington passed on to the eldest son Richard, and Richard, who was only six years older than his cousin Laurence, "became a father" to him. Richard agreed to contribute thirty pounds a year toward the expense of the university, and with this aid Laurence was admitted as a sizar to Jesus College, Cambridge, on July 6, 1733.

In his memoir Sterne says nothing regarding his studies at Cambridge. It is probable that there was very little out of the ordinary in his career as a student, and nothing that stamped itself with indelible force upon his memory. A year after his admission as a sizar he was elected to one of the six scholarships established through the benefactions of his great-grandfather the Archbishop. There were some irregularities here, inasmuch as the funds were intended only for natives of Yorkshire and Nottinghamshire. However, it is probable that his cousin Richard and his uncle Jaques, who had been educated in Jesus College and was already well known in the church circles at York, intervened in his behalf to overcome these technical difficulties. At Cambridge Sterne readily learned the advantages of being endowed with the right name.

At any rate, he was named on July 30, 1734, as a beneficiary to one of the scholarships and studied until January, 1736, when he was admitted to the degree of Bachelor of Arts. This much, at least, the record shows. While he has been accused of paying slight attention to his studies, the record would indicate that he was certainly no worse in that respect than the average student of his time. He passed through the course prescribed for him by his tutors in the usual length of time and had no difficulty in being admitted to his degree.

However, we can judge from *Tristram Shandy* what his attitude toward the university life and learning must have been. The elder Shandy, with his systems and theories, his reasonings and syllogisms, was Sterne's ridicule of the logicians who dominated the academic thought of the time. The important thing was not the conclusion, but the formal logic by which one arrived at the conclusion—not the product of reasoning, but the words that were used in setting forth the reasoning. Indeed, Sterne seemed already to understand that the era of pompous metaphysics, of logic for the sake of logic, was on its way out. A new spirit in learning was beginning to make itself felt—a spirit that had less to do with books and words and scholastic dispute and more to do with the practical needs and desires of humanity. The world had emerged from its shell of superstition and slavish subjugation to the classical precepts. Scientists were beginning to break the chains of ignorance and religious demagogy; the first faint rumblings of democratic thought—which would find fruition in France and America—had already been heard, in the writings of Locke and others.

It was to Locke that Sterne turned as a guiding light to lead him out of the academic bog. In the *Essay on Human Understanding* he found relief from the obscure pomposities of a large part of formal education. Later, when Sterne had become famous, he alluded often to Locke in terms of highest regard.

The tradition long existed and in fact is still widely current among students of Sterne that in his three years at the university he gained a reputation as a member of a notorious group; that he was lazy; and, in fact, that he was something of a rake. No evidence has been presented to support this tradition; on the contrary, he seems to have had no reputation at all, for few of his fellow students seem to have remembered him as a student in later years. Gray, the gentle author of the *Elegy in the Country Churchyard*, who was at Cambridge at the same time, spoke of Sterne after he had become famous, but he does not mention ever having heard of Sterne as a student. One contemporary, writing of Sterne after *Tristram Shandy* had made him famous, recalled that Sterne was known as "odd" and was sometimes puzzling to his tutors, but of no harm. These facts hardly support the tradition of the notorious rake.

The idea seems to have arisen largely out of the fact that Sterne struck up a friendship here with John Hall, who later married and added the name Stevenson to his own. Hall-Stevenson may have been all the things that Sterne was credited with being. Even in the university this young man gained the reputation of *bon vivant* and confirmed roué. Later in life, as master of the famous Skelton Castle, which he renamed Crazy Castle, he gathered about him a group of gay companions, who gained notoriety as the "Demoniacs."

Sterne, in his memoir, says in his terse unadorned manner, " 'Twas there that I commenced a friendship with Mr. H—, which has been lasting on both sides." His friendship for Hall-Stevenson was indeed the most lasting thing in Sterne's life. To him Sterne addressed the most intimate letters, writing to him as "Cousin Anthony"; he became the Eugenius, Yorick's counselor, of *Tristram Shandy*. Long after both men had left the university behind them, when Hall-Stevenson had become the master of Crazy Castle, Sterne often left his parsonage to visit the old structure, to drink and be gay with the Demoniacs, or revel in the great library with its many volumes of *litera curiosa*.

A portrait of John Hall-Stevenson shows him as a very handsome man, without that sensitiveness of features that characterized Sterne, but with keen eyes and a sardonic expression about a rather sensuous mouth and chin. There can be little doubt that women found him attractive, and he probably did not neglect to take his advantage as he found it. He had a failing which followed him through a long life: a tendency to hypochondria. He was fully convinced that an east wind was the cause of his disorders and illnesses, and when the wind was in the east he would retire to his bedroom until the unlucky breeze had shifted.

Sterne's association with Hall-Stevenson could hardly have borne any other result than to add to the parson's ill fame. Hall-Stevenson's tastes in literature, as well as in living, sought the lower levels, and his notoriety reached a climax in 1762, when he published a volume of stories in verse called *Crazy Tales*. The book went further in its humor than even the depraved tastes of the age condoned, and the author was heartily damned in some quarters. Sterne was suspected of authorship of some portions of the book, and much of the condemnation fell on his head.

Many of Sterne's contemporaries and practically all of his biographers have deplored his friendship for Hall-Stevenson. Yet in drawing an estimation of the man Sterne a significant fact can not be overlooked: his capacity for friendship was tested through more than thirty years of intimacy with Hall-Stevenson. Whatever the companionship may have been on the part of his dissolute friend, on Sterne's part at least it was sincere and firm. When it might have been to the author's advantage to disavow his association with the lord of Skelton, he instead maintained the friendship on the most intimate terms until his death. While this does not indicate any sacrifice or nobility on Sterne's part, still he was wise enough to realize the public disadvantages of his association with Hall-Stevenson and be governed accordingly. And from a literary point of view his association with Hall-Stevenson is even more important, for without it the world might never have had *Tristram Shandy*.

It was Hall-Stevenson who directed Sterne's reading into unholy channels. He introduced Sterne into the realm of strange and often indelicate humor of which Rabelais was the most famous practitioner and of which there were many more infamous ones. It was in Hall-Stevenson's library that Sterne found many of the strange whims of typography, pagination, and style, as well as suggestions for many of the stories and allusions that are part and parcel of *Tristram Shandy*.

The foundation for the extensive reading that went into the making of *Tristram Shandy* was undoubtedly laid at the university, under the guidance of Hall-Stevenson. We can see the two men sitting together over a bottle of wine, with Hall-Stevenson's Rabelais before them. The *rapport* between the two young men was perfect; there was something in the nature of each that was keenly adjusted to the other. The letters that Sterne wrote to his "cousin Anthony" are unlike any other letters from his pen. There is an intimacy that was complete; to Hall-Stevenson Sterne often revealed thoughts and feelings that remained hidden from others, and many of the letters show a friendly concern that gives us an insight into one phase of Sterne's character.

In the course of his career at the university, Sterne also met an adversary destined to follow him through life—a disease which lurked in his frail chest. His father's babies had all been born with perilously weak constitutions, and the hardships of travel and a childhood life in the army camps had contributed to their frailty. Four had died in infancy, and the one remaining son was destined to spend his life in a difficult struggle against an opponent from which there was no escape. In the last year of his study at Cambridge he awoke one night to find that he had bled "the bed full" from a hemorrhage of the lungs.

It is a tribute to Sterne's character that even the terrible malady with which he learned he was afflicted could not overcome him. Through life he allowed himself to be "treated" with the preposterous cures invented by a baffled medical science. But in every instance physicians failed and Sterne found himself thrown on his own resources. He met every onslaught of the disease with courage and a jest, leading Death "a dance he little thinks of." Time after time he saw the shadow of Death over his bed, and with admirable fortitude conquered his adversary and lived to write another day. In fact, the idea of his jesting in the face of death became so much a part of the Sterne tradition that upon his death it was commonly accepted that he had been gay to the very end. A biographical sketch written sixty years after his end contains this typical expression:

> He died as he lived. A day or two before he seemed not in the least affected by the prospect of his approaching dissolution.

Aside from his friendship for John Hall-Stevenson, one other university association is worth noting here, because of its importance in the future. At Cambridge Sterne met John Fountayne, who like the humorist was destined for the church. Fountayne later became Dean of York, in which position he was able to aid Sterne. The incident, which will be considered in a later chapter, gave rise to a pamphlet in which Sterne first showed unusual promise as a satirical writer.

Sterne nowhere indicates his reason for choosing the church as a career, and it is more than likely that he chose it as a matter of convenience. His great-grandfather had been Archbishop of York, and his uncle was currently powerful in the cathedral circle of York. His chances for preferment, under such conditions, seemed excellent, and consequently Sterne directed his studies with a church career in view.

In January, 1736, after two and a half years in residence, Sterne was admitted to the degree of Bachelor of Arts, and left the university. Four years later he was admitted to the Master's degree.

IV

A Sentimental Romance

IN MARCH, 1736, only a few weeks after Sterne left the university, he took his place in the church, as curate to the vicar of St. Ives. But he had only a short apprenticeship to serve, for his uncle Jaques came to his aid. The exact time that he was at St. Ives is not known, but it could not have been more than two years, for we have the record of a special ordination service held at Chester on August 20, 1738, at which the young man was admitted into the priesthood. Shortly afterward he was appointed to the living of Sutton-in-the-Forest, which later came under the ecclesiastic jurisdiction of his uncle Jaques, as Archdeacon of Cleveland.

The village of Sutton and the land around it which comprised Sterne's vicarage had little to attract a spirited young man. Much of the twenty square miles over which he was given guardianship was heavily wooded and very sparsely populated. With an assistant to look after the business of the parish, Sterne was content to spend most of his time at York, the center of local church government. He visited Sutton for Sunday services, or when some special business required his attention, but young men seeking church preferment found it expedient to stay close to the seat of power—in Sterne's case, York. The living of Sutton brought in forty pounds a year, on which the young vicar could live in some degree of comfort, and he sought higher favor in the church by aiding his uncle.

Meanwhile he prepared for his Master's degree, and in July, 1740, the degree was granted by the university. Church preferment was not far behind, and several months later he secured a prebend in the York Cathedral, which added forty pounds a year to his income. Another minor prebend, which brought in ten pounds, gave him a total income of some ninety pounds a year. At twenty-six, Sterne already held three ecclesiastic offices, preached in his turn at York, and seemed well on his way to great preferment. He might have become a pluralist to rival his uncle Jaques, who held innumerable offices; however, a combination of character and circumstances kept him from advancing far in the church.

But a much more important event had occurred in the young vicar's life. He had fallen in love.

The woman with whom Sterne was carrying on a courtship was Elizabeth Lumley, a cousin of Elizabeth Montagu, London's famous Bluestocking arbiter. Although a woman of good family and social grace, she was something less than amiable, if we can trust the comments of many who knew her well. Mrs. Montagu herself called her cousin a "fretful porcupine," and an exchange of letters between Mrs. Montagu and her brother refers to the "arm of flesh," with which she was expected to subdue the young vicar of Sutton.

A crayon portrait of her by Frances Cotes shows her as a proud and haughty woman, rather plump of face, with thick features and a large nose. As her cousin suggested, it was not her beauty by which she could hope to tame Laurence Sterne.

Nevertheless, Sterne was charmed by her. In his memoir, written after years of estrangement, he recalled:

> .... at York, I became acquainted with your mother
> and courted her for two years:—she owned she liked
> me; but thought herself not rich enough, or me too
> poor, to be joined together.—She went to her sister's
> in S—; and I wrote to her often.—I believe she was
> partly determined to have me, but would not say
> so.—At her return she fell into a consumption;—and
> one evening that I was sitting by her, with an almost
> broken heart to see her so ill, she said, "My dear
> Laurey, I never can be yours, for I verily believe I
> have not long to live! but I have left you every shilling of my fortune." Upon that she showed me her
> will.—This generosity overpowered me.—It pleased
> God that she recovered, and I married her in the
> year 1741.

Sterne met Elizabeth Lumley late in 1738, after he had become the vicar of Sutton. He was in his twenty-fifth year, and Miss Lumley was about the same age. In a period when women married early, she was approaching the fatal age of the old maid's cap; and to add to her discomfiture, a younger sister had already married a promising young churchman. Several years before she met Sterne, Miss Lumley had come into a small estate, the income from which was about thirty pounds a year, a considerable income for a young unmarried woman. There seems to be little doubt that she set her cap for the young vicar, and as soon as financial circumstances permitted, she married him.

The courtship lasted more than two years, and it is interesting as the first "sentimental" romance on record. No one had ever before used the word "sentimental," but before Sterne's death his writings had given it a wide usage in English and had forced French and German translators to synthesize words to carry over the meaning. The word was used by Sterne to characterize his work, and he has been too often loosely described as a "sentimentalist." However, the word as applied to literature today has been corrupted in meaning and has gained a sophomoric connotation that Sterne would not have relished; it will be seen that in the current sense of the word Sterne was not a "sentimentalist."

Sterne called on Miss Lumley often at her apartment in York. The city was a center of gaiety and social life; its theatres, concert halls and races attracted throngs in which were included many great names of the period. The tall, slender young vicar and the proud Miss Lumley were often among these gay crowds in the concert halls and theatres. They sat together over dinner; sometimes they drove or took long walks together. So two years of courtship passed, Sterne professing his love, and the practical young woman adding the total of their incomes dubiously.

At about the time that Sterne was being admitted to the Master's degree, thus strengthening his prospect of preferment, Elizabeth left York to visit her married sister in Staffordshire. The visit stretched out into several months, and Sterne, "languishing" for her presence, wrote often to her. It is in the letters that have come down to us that we get a picture of the romance, and the evidence seems to indicate a romance more of the head than of the heart. They are not the letters of a man carried away by passion, as the journal written to Eliza Draper many years later certainly was; there is a studied play of words, an artful lovemaking here. This is not to say that Sterne's love was not sincere; but there are many varieties of love and many gradations of passion. Sterne's love for Elizabeth Lumley was a love assiduously cultivated; she was the horticulturist who planted seeds of love and reaped studied phrases.

There may have been more than accident in the long vacation, for absence ripens many a romance, and Elizabeth Lumley was a wise gardener. The first letter is more an impersonal essay on love than the passion of a "languishing" heart:

> Yes! I will steal from the world, and not a babbling tongue shall tell where I am,—Echo shall not so much as whisper my hiding place,—suffer thy imagination to paint it at a little sun-gilt cottage, on the side of a romantic hill;—dost thou think I will leave love and friendship behind me? No! they shall be my companions in solitude, for they will sit down and rise up with me in the amiable form of my L——. We will be as merry and as innocent as our first parents in Paradise, before the arch-fiend entered that undescribable scene.
>
> The kindest affections will have room to shoot and expand in our retirement, and produce such fruit as madness, and envy, and ambition, have always killed in the bud.—Let the human tempest and hurricane rage at a distance, the desolation is beyond the horizon of peace.—My L. has seen a polyanthus blow in December,—some friendly wall has sheltered it from the biting wind.—No planetary influence shall reach us, but that which presides and cherishes the sweetest flowers.—God preserve us! how delightful this prospect in idea! We will build and we will plant in our own way,—simplicity shall not be tortured by art,—we will learn of Nature how to live,—she shall be our alchymist to mingle all the good of life into one salubrious draught.—The gloomy family of care and distrust shall be banished from our dwelling, guarded by thy kind and tutelary deity;—we will sing our choral songs of gratitude, and rejoice to the end of our pilgrimage.
>
> Adieu, my L. Return to one who languishes for thy society.

The essay is pretty enough, but the wise Miss Lumley

detected its impersonal note. The ground she had planted needed more spade work. So she prompted him with questions; she asked how he was tormented by her leaving; she reminded him of their days together by asking about the cottage of a mutual friend, which they had named D'Estella, after a lover's fancy. And Sterne, quick to take the prompting, turned his phrases on a less formal note:

You bid me tell you, my dear L., how I bore your departure for S——, and whether the valley where D'Estella stands, retains still its looks,—or if I think the roses or jessamines smell as sweet, as when you left it.—Alas! everything has now lost its relish and look! The hour you left D'Estella, I took to my bed.—I was worn out with fevers of all kinds, but most by that fever of the heart with which thou knowest well I have been wasting these two years— and shall continue wasting until you quit S——. The good Miss S——, from the forebodings of the best of hearts, thinking I was ill, insisted upon my going to her. . . . She made me stay an hour with her, and in that short space, I burst into tears a dozen different times—and in such affectionate gusts of passion, that she was constrained to leave the room,—and sympa- thize in her dressing-room—I have been weeping for you both, said she, in a tone of the sweetest pity,— for poor L's heart, I have long known it—her anguish is as sharp as yours,—her heart as tender,—her constancy as great,—her virtues as heroic;—Heaven brought you not together to be tormented. I could only answer her with a kind look, and a heavy sigh,— and returned home to your lodgings (which I had hired till your return) to resign myself to misery.— Fanny had prepared me a supper,—she is all attention to me;—but I sat over it with tears; a bitter sauce, my L., but I could eat with no other:—for the moment she began to spread my little table, my heart fainted within me.—One solitary plate, one knife, one fork, one glass!—I gave a thousand penetrating looks at the chair which thou hadst so often graced, in those quiet and sentimental repasts,—

This was more pleasing to Miss Lumley, for it indicated that the seeds sown by her absence were bearing fruit. Yet she had occasion later in the course of her absence to upbraid her young lover for his neglect of her, and Sterne wrote to apologize, in as artificial an essay as can be discovered in the whole catalogue of love:

Before now my L. has lodged an indictment against me in the high court of friendship;—I plead guilty to the charge, and entirely submit to the mercy of that amiable tribunal.—Let this mitigate my punishment, if it will not expiate my transgression,—do not say that I shall offend again in the same manner, though a too easy pardon sometimes occasions a repetition of the same fault.—A miser says, Though I do no good with my money today, tomorrow shall be marked with some deed of beneficence.—The Libertine says, Let me enjoy this week in forbidden and luxurious pleasures, and the next I will dedicate to serious thought and reflection.—The Gamester says, Let me have one more chance with the dice, and I will never touch them more.—The Knave of every profession wishes to obtain but independency, and he will become an honest man.—The female Coquette triumphs in tormenting her enamorato, for fear, after marriage, he should not pity her.

My L.!—thou art surrounded by all the melancholy gloom of winter! wert thou alone, the retirement would be agreeable,—disappointed ambition might envy such a retreat, and disappointed love would seek it out.—Crowded towns, and busy societies, may delight the unthinking and gay—but solitude is the best nurse of wisdom.—Methinks I see my contemplative girl in the garden, watching the gradual approaches of spring.—Dost not thou mark with delight the first vernal buds of the snow-drop and primrose, these

early and welcome visitors, spring beneath thy feet.—
Flora and Pomona already consider thee as their
handmaid, and a little time will load thee with their
sweetest blessing.—The feathered race are all thy
own, and with them, untaught harmony will soon
begin to cheer thy morning and evening walks.—
Sweet as this may be, return—return—the birds of
Yorkshire will tune their pipes, and sing as melodi-
ously as those of Staffordshire.

    Adieu, my beloved L.; thine too much for my
peace.

And still once again Miss Lumley's pride was offended
by Sterne's neglect, and again he wrote to apologize. But
the spring was coming, and a long winter's separation
neared its end.

In the spring of 1741, the lovers were reunited. Their
status, financially, had in the meantime changed for the
better. Sterne had received the prebend stall in York
cathedral, with its forty pounds annually, and Elizabeth's
income had more than doubled, as the result of a legacy
from a distant relative. Presumably the young lady had
no further qualms about the matter of income; she was
about twenty-seven years old, and she may well have been
anxious for the marriage so near her grasp.

Soon after she returned to York, she became ill, as
Sterne later recalled. The scene in her sick-room, in
which she showed her young lover the will naming him
as beneficiary of her estates, was no doubt touching. Yet
a clearer appraisal of the incident shows more method in
it than may at first be apparent. Her illness seems to
have been somewhat less than fatal, for she outlived Sterne
himself by several years, but nothing could have been better calculated to work on the young clergyman's sympathies than the practical demonstration of her love contained in her will.

If she hoped this would bring the courtship to a head, her hopes were not far from realization. Sterne avowed himself "overcome," and when Miss Lumley recovered, it was she who suggested marriage. On March 30, 1741, the lovers were married at York, with the Dean reading the service.

The exchange of letters between Mrs. Montagu and her brother, in which the marriage is discussed, throws an interesting light on Sterne's reputation and his wife's character. ". . . . our cousin Betty Lumley," Matthew Robinson wrote his sister from Bath, "is married to a Parson who once delighted in debauchery, who is possessed of about £100 a year in preferment, and has a good prospect of more. What hopes our relation may have of settling the affections of a light and fickle man I know not, but I imagine she will set about it not by means of the beauty but of the arm of flesh. In other respects I see no fault in the match; no woman ought to venture upon the state of Old Maiden without a consciousness of an inexhaustible fund of good nature." In a letter to her sister, passing on the family gossip, Mrs. Montagu said casually of Sterne, that "He was a great rake, but, being japanned and married, has varnished his character."

Sterne's courtship and marriage give a clear picture of the man's character. His commentators have long argued the moot question of how much was real and how much unreal in his professed love for his wife; one may as well ask how much of life is real and how much unreal, for his love was surely as real as anything that ever happened to Sterne. It is one of the paradoxes of the man's life that, despite his ready tears, love never touched him deeply. His love for Eliza Draper came near to unloosing a flood of passion, but it was a passion he played with, never really believing his love would be fulfilled. As for the rest—

Elizabeth Lumley, Catherine de Fourmantelle, Lady Percy, and the others—they form only a background in the tapestry of Sterne's life. He must forever have "some Dulcinea" in his mind, to torment his thoughts. But the Dulcineas never deeply tormented his emotions.

It is axiomatic that love is often a matter of circumstances; more marriages are made on earth than in heaven; Sterne's case offers eloquent proof. Consider all the elements in Elizabeth Lumley's favor. She was a woman of good family and high connections. Her income made her a good match for a man of moderate means. Local church officials would look with approval on such a marriage and would certainly be more inclined to favor the young clergyman with advancement if he were settled well with a woman of unimpeachable name. With all these things in her favor, what did it matter that she was a humorless shrew, certainly not the sort of woman who could settle the irrepressible Yorick?

Sterne surely felt a sort of love for Elizabeth Lumley. Yet there is more than a little evidence to indicate that he entered matrimony with something less than enthusiasm. Had he wished it, he might certainly have brought the long courtship to a head months earlier. It is more likely that, once caught in the tide of his "love affair," he permitted himself to be carried along without resistance. It is even possible that his uncle Jaques may have urged the marriage, and Sterne allowed his advantage to color his love.

This would seem to fit in well with Sterne's character as we see it at the time. He had not yet, at the age of twenty-seven, developed for himself a clear philosophy of life. He was content to drift with the tide, accepting whatever was to his advantage, and not scrupling too much over the cost. He had accepted the aid of his uncle

Jaques, knowing that his uncle would expect political assistance in return; during these years he did his uncle's bidding, despite the fact that the churchman's opinions must have clashed sharply with his own on many occasions.

Mrs. Montagu's description of Sterne as a rake is not to be taken without a leaven. It is Sterne's misfortune—or good fortune—that he earned the reputation of the character without the joys. More than a small part of the reputation was no doubt traceable to his association with the notorious Hall-Stevenson, and to his reading tastes, which must have been considered unorthodox for a country parson, even in those days. Despite Sterne's ever-changing Dulcineas, his amorous adventures were hardly great enough to have earned him the reputation of a roué. Sterne loved women, but his love was often more abstract than practical. A dilettante of love he may have been—a philanderer, even—but a rake, hardly.

V

The Parson at Home

STERNE nowhere refers very definitely to the events of the next few years, and the records are meagre. The couple gave up their separate lodgings at York and took over the parsonage of Sutton-in-the-Forest, which Sterne had never occupied since his appointment to the living, three years before.

But it was a sorry home to which he brought his young bride. Having been occupied previously by a poor clergyman, the house was allowed to fall into a sad state of repair. Work was begun immediately, but it took some time to repair the chimneys, floors, and the decayed plastering. Sterne, disgusted at the expense, entered in his register a complaint which might have come from the pen of Walter Shandy himself:

A. Dom. 1741

Laid out in sashing the house	12 0 0
In stuckoing and bricking the hall	4 6 0
In building the chair-house	5 0 0
In building the parlor chimney	3 0 0

Spent in shaping the rooms, plastering, underdrawing, and jobbing, God knows how much!

The repairs were at last completed, and the chair-house was built for Mrs. Sterne's carriage. The house was completely refurnished, to the taste of its new occupants, and Sterne prepared to settle down in this scene of rural domesticity.

The first months must have been pleasant enough for the young parson. He began to plan the arrangement of the grounds and gardens. His notes recorded the planting of apple, peach, pear, plum and cherry trees. The orchard was enclosed, an arbor built, and elm trees were planted in the churchyard and garden. Here, among trees that he had set himself, among the "pleasing walks" that he had planned, Sterne was to spend the twenty years which intervened before he burst full-blown upon the horizon of literary England.

Most of Sterne's biographers believe that sometime, either just before or just after his marriage, Sterne traveled on the Continent, making the "grand tour" as governor to the young Earl of Aboyne. As evidence they cite Yorick's complaint in *Tristram Shandy* of the asthma he had caught skating against the wind in Flanders; certain passages indicating Sterne's early familiarity with the French terrain and finally Yorick's reflection:

> I had just time, in my travels through *Denmark* with Mr. *Noddy's* eldest son, whom, in the year 1741, I accompanied as governor, riding along with him at a prodigious rate, thro' most parts of *Europe,* and of which original journey performed by us two, a most delectable narrative will be given in the course of this work; I had just time, I say, and that was all, to prove the truth of an observation, made by a long sojourner in that country;—namely, "that nature was neither very lavish, nor was she very stingy in her gifts of genius and capacity to its inhabitants."

Despite this evidence, however, it is very unlikely that Sterne traveled on the Continent in 1741. The series of letters written to Elizabeth Lumley, and his own account of her illness in the early spring of that year are conclusive proof that he could not have done so just before his marriage. After his marriage he was occupied with redecorating his new home and planning the gardens. An entry in his register, remarkable for its Gargantuan quality, indicates that he spent the summer in England:

> Hail fell in the midst of summer as large as a pigeon's egg, which unusual Occurrence I thought fit to attest under my own hand.

And finally, Sterne must have been in England in the late autumn of 1741, for in December a more desirable prebend stall in York Cathedral became vacant and Sterne received the appointment. At the most there is a period of about three months not fully accounted for. Assuming that he could have traveled through Europe at a "prodigious rate" during those months, it does not seem probable that he would have left his wife or the seething political cauldron of the cathedral circle at this particular period. The remarkable knowledge of the French terrain and continental scenes that he exhibits in *Tristram Shandy* are not the glimpses caught on a flying trip and remembered twenty years later; it is rather the result of a wide reading; possibly the battle-ground scenes were based on accounts given him as a child by his father. The autobiographical elements in *Tristram Shandy* are to be found more in the characters, opinions, and attitudes than in the narration of events.

Sterne entered with enthusiasm into the life of a country squire, and on land he acquired he experimented in farming. Sterne purchased livestock, including seven cows and a flock of geese; his land he planted to barley and oats. But from a financial point of view, his farming ventures were complete failures. As though afflicted themselves with Shandean impulses, his geese wandered unconfined; the butter was sold too cheaply, for Mrs. Sterne (in whose charge the dairy department lay) evidently had no more business acumen than her husband; and the crops, despite all of Sterne's experiments, failed to pay for their keep. In 1767, long after he had put his farming days behind him, Sterne wrote in a jocular mood:

> —You are much to blame if you dig for marl, unless you are sure of it. I was once such a puppy myself, as to pare, and burn, and had my labor for my pains, and two hundred pounds out of my pocket. Curse on farming (said I) I will try if the pen will not succeed better than the spade. The following up of that affair (I mean farming) made me lose my temper: and a cart-load of turnips was (I thought) very dear at two hundred pounds.
>
> In all your operations, may your own good sense guide you! Bought experience is the Devil.—Adieu, adieu.—

The "bought experience" which proved so costly was made possible by two appointments in the church. The first, already mentioned, was the prebend of North Newbald, to which Sterne was appointed several months after his marriage. This prebend brought in forty pounds a year and in addition brought to its holder a house in York. The second appointment, which Sterne secured through his wife, was to the living of Stillington, a village about two miles from Sutton, which included the prebend and was also worth forty pounds a year. Lord Fairfax had promised Elizabeth Lumley that if she married a Yorkshire clergyman, he would present her husband with the living, which was in his gift. A special order was required to permit Sterne to hold both the living of Sutton and of Stillington, setting Sterne well on his way to becoming a minor pluralist.

From his prebends and two parishes, combined with his wife's income, Sterne now had about two hundred pounds a year, and he could afford to live comfortably, purchase land and pay for his experience as a farmer. His life during these years was the life of the conventional churchman or landowner. His interests lay in the countryside—in the people of his parish, in lands and markets. From all evidence, his thoughts and writings of this period were equally conventional. A fragment of verse, which he called *The Unknown,* written upon "hearing a Pass-bell," reflects on the mystery of death and immortality of the soul. Its style is quaint, but typical of poetry of this kind, while its approach to the age-old mysteries on which it reflected certainly was conventional enough. It began:

> Harke my gay Friend that solemn Toll
> Speaks ye departure of a soul;
> 'Tis gone, that's all we know—not where
> Or how ye unbody'd soul do's fare—
> In that mysterious world none knows,
> But God alone to whom it goes;
> To whom departed souls return
> To take their doom to smile or mourn.

But occasionally, even then, the author of *Tristram Shandy* asserted himself through the surface of Parson Sterne. He could not resist an occasional Shandean joke within the precincts of his parish register. The summer storm in which hailstones as large as a "pigeon's egg" fell (!) was exceeded in 1745; in spite of the losses which Sterne suffered, he had humor enough to record this meteorological wonder:

In May, 1745, a dismal storm of hail fell upon this town, and upon some other adjacent ones, which did considerable damage both to the windows and corn. Many of the stones measured six inches in circumference. It broke almost all the south and west windows, both of this house and my vicarage at Stillington.

In fact, his sense of humor was gaining for him something of a reputation as a local wit. He was well known in York, having spent three years there and spending much time there even after his marriage. Numerous anecdotes and traditions that grew up in York date to this period, and show Sterne as a man of ready retort. An anecdote which attained wider prominence than any of the others concerns a young officer who, having drunk too freely, was regaling his friends in a York coffee house with a fund of broad stories. Sterne was sitting at a table with a friend, and when the young officer saw him, he began a loud abuse of the clergy. Sterne listened with amused tolerance, then told the young officer about his father's dog.

"He had a dog—a very fine dog to all appearance—but he had one fault. Whenever he saw a clergyman, he would always snarl at him."

"Pray, how long has he had that trick?" the young soldier asked.

"Why, sir," answered Sterne, "ever since he was a *puppy!*"

According to tradition, Sterne's retort carried the day and the young officer retired, completely downed.

He gained some popularity as a "preacher" also. A contemporary note reveals that he was at best an indifferent orator, and that when he spoke many of the congregation arose and left the church. In spite of this, however, he was favored by many; his sermons, if those later published are a fair sample of what he was writing at this early period, abound in happy expressions. Often he turned his text paradoxically, to end with a moral at complete variance with the words of the text—which must have proved amusing to the more intelligent part of his congregations. He had, furthermore, a wide acquaintance with the published sermons of famous clergymen, and he did not hesitate to borrow ideas, or even complete phrases, when they suited his needs. In all fairness to him, however, it must be reported that the manuscripts of many of his sermons, examined after his death, contain notations as to the source of "borrowed" material. It is evident that concealed plagiarism was not his intention.

His sermons, he wrote to Eliza Draper many years later, "came all hot from the heart." The best of his sermons are forthright pieces, frank and with more honesty than one expects in essays designed for the church. And they were intensely personal: Sterne praised the things of life which he most honored, and he often interpreted his texts from an extremely practical point of view. He must have set a congregation on edge when he began, on the text, *It is better to go to a house of mourning than to the house of feasting:*

> That I deny—but let us hear the wise man's reasoning upon it—*for that* is *the end of all men, and the living* will *lay it to* his *heart: sorrow is better than laughter*—for a crack-brain'd order of Carthusian monks, I grant, but not for men of the world: For what purpose, do you imagine, has God made us? for the social sweets of the well-watered valleys, where he has planted us, or for the dry and dismal desert of a *Sierra Morena?* Are the sad accidents of life, and the uncheery hours which perpetually overtake us, are they not enough, but we must sally forth in quest of them,—belie our own hearts, and say as our text would have us, that they are better than those of joy?—

It was the custom for prebendaries who found it inconvenient to preach at York when their turns came to secure substitutes at their own expense. Sterne was able to add substantially to his income by preaching as a substitute for his brother prebendaries. This fact brought out an interesting correspondence several years later, when Sterne had broken with his uncle Jaques.

The entries in the parish register for 1745 record with touching brevity a tragedy in the lives of Sterne and his wife. On October 1, Sterne made this entry:

> Baptised in 1745. Oct. ye 1st.—Born and baptised Lydia, the daughter of the Reverend Mr. Sterne and of Elizabeth his wife, daughter of the Rev. Mr. Lumley, late Rector of Bedel.

And on the very next day he entered its sad sequel:

> Burials, 1745. Oct. 2—Lydia, daughter of Mr. Sterne, Vicar of Sutton.

The child whose visit on this earth was so short was named Lydia for Mrs. Sterne's younger sister. They had determined to call their child, if it was a girl, by this name, and when, two years later, another child was born to them, she was also named Lydia.

This was the daughter who was to occupy the foremost place in Sterne's heart throughout the years of his life. His letters, when she had grown to young womanhood, were full of pride in his "elegant, accomplished little slut." When the time came for parting from her—a parting which was to be his last—he wrote to a friend, "My heart bleeds, L——, when I think of parting with my child;—'twill be like the separation of soul and body,—and equal to nothing but what passes at that tremendous moment." For her he "could get fast up the hill of preferment, if I chose it;—but without my Lydia, if a mitre was offered me, it would sit uneasy upon my brow." It is through Lydia that we get a glimpse of the real Sterne under the jester's gay colors. But Lydia was a daughter of her father, and like him, she was to prove errant and unstable.

VI

The Demoniacs of Crazy Castle

"As to the Squire of the parish," Sterne wrote in the
memoir to his daughter, "I can not say we were upon a
very friendly footing." Thus did he commemorate the
long-standing unpleasantness between him and Philip Harland. Although it never broke into an open quarrel, still
this difference was strong enough and open enough so
that the villagers of Sutton took sides, either for the parson
or for the squire. It was bitter enough to account for
several of the bitterest passages in *Tristram Shandy,* and
in the division of his parishioners, it must be admitted
that Sterne took something the worst of it. His lack of
popularity is shown in an anecdote, which tells of Sterne's
narrow escape from an icy death. The parson had gone
skating on the pond in Stillington Common, as was his
custom. When the ice gave way, he was plunged into the
cold water; he shouted and waved his arms wildly, but
none of the bystanders would aid him, because of their
enmity. So goes the story, and whether the details are
accurate or not, it at least serves to indicate the lack of
sympathy between the villagers and the young clergyman.

The reason for this unpopularity may have been Sterne's
ill-advised venture in dairying. Mrs. Sterne undersold her
neighbors, and it is not difficult to understand how this

would have resulted in friction at a time when such practice was a legal offense. As for the differences between Sterne and Squire Harland, no definite cause has ever been assigned for them. Perhaps political differences caused a friction, but it is more probable that it was merely a case of friction in personalities. Sterne disliked the proud landowner, with his high manner and family worship, and it is more than probable that Harland resented the easygoing, jesting ways of the parson.

But in opposition to this, the Sternes found warm friends in the Crofts of Stillington Hall. Stephen Croft, a descendant of Christopher Croft, one-time Lord Mayor of York, had engaged in a profitable wine trade. On the death of his father, he had inherited the Stillington estates, and he brought his wife to live in the great hall. Throughout the remainder of his life, Sterne maintained the most friendly relations with Croft, and they exchanged correspondence after Sterne had become a famous and much sought-after man of letters. A note to Croft from London described the political state of affairs in the early sixties.

From Sterne's letters during his early years at Sutton, we catch glimpses of the Sternes going to Stillington as dinner guests. We see the two men and their wives sitting before the great fire, discussing village affairs, books, politics. The two men were of about the same age, with many interests and opinions in common. Croft could enjoy a jest as well as the clergyman could, and they spent many merry evenings together. It was to the Crofts that Sterne carried the first chapters of *Tristram Shandy,* and an anecdote survives to recall how much Sterne owed to Croft's friendship. It was said that when Sterne had finished reading his manuscript, he detected—or thought he detected—a cool response among his little audience. Disgusted with his brain-child, Sterne hurled the sheets into the grate; Croft stepped forward and snatched the manuscript in the split-second before it caught fire, saving the work of genius for the world.

Of all the friendships that Sterne was to form, however, none quite matched his intimacy with the much-berated John Hall-Stevenson. After leaving the university without a degree, Hall had traveled on the Continent, as was the custom among wealthy young men at the time. On his return to England in 1740, he married Anne Stevenson, and added her name to his own. He was already the master of Skelton Castle, which had come to him when his father died, and he settled down into an easy life at Skelton. Only once was he jostled out of his easy existence. In 1745, the Stuart pretender, "Prince Charlie," landed in Scotland, and marched against England to reclaim the throne from the Hanover George II. Hall formed a company of cavalry and took an active part in the campaign against the invader. When the insurrection had been put down, Hall returned to Skelton to take up his life of comfort again, and from that time on he allowed nothing to disturb the serenity of his life in the gloomy old castle.

Hall carried with him through life his love of books, and he delighted especially in volumes of curious humor. His rich library contained many of these books, with which he had a wide acquaintance, and the young man entertained himself by writing occasional verse, or a satirical pamphlet, which he published anonymously and which amused many of his contemporaries.

Skelton Hall was the sort of manor our Hollywood producers like to give us in their weird mystery movies. As shown in the frontispiece of Hall-Stevenson's *Crazy Tales*, it stands against a background of hills, rising high over its heavy-walled battlements. A gloomy turret, over which

blew a "thin, death-doing, pestiferous north-east wind,"
stands to the right of the main structure, its towers rising
several stories above the rest of the castle—perhaps the
prison stronghold of some medieval lord.

The castle had belonged to Lawson Trotter, Hall-Stevenson's uncle. Trotter, who was noted for his Jacobite
leanings, perhaps felt the castle to be an encumbrance.
At any rate, he sold it to his brother, Hall-Stevenson's
father, at whose death it passed to the young man. It is
interesting to mention in passing that the insurrection of
1745, in which Hall-Stevenson left his fortress to fight for
the Hanovers, forced Trotter to flee from England because
of his sympathies with the cause of the pretender prince.
He went into exile in France, and when Sterne in the
course of his residence in France met him and showed him
the picture of the castle in *Crazy Tales*, Trotter was overjoyed.

When young Hall-Stevenson took up his life in the
castle, he renamed it—from a whim in keeping with his
character—Crazy Castle. Here he lived, week in and week
out, leaving it only for a trip to London, to York for the
races, or to Scarborough for the waters. He spent much
time in his large library, or entertained his friends in the
castle.

The strong relationship between Sterne and Hall-Stevenson may have waned in the first years of the parson's
married life. Hall-Stevenson had been traveling on the
Continent, and when he returned, the paths of the two
men were widely divergent. But there was a common
bond that drew them together, and it is certain that within
a few years after the campaign of 1745, the friendship had
been renewed faster than ever before. Sterne spent much
time with Hall-Stevenson in the library at Crazy Castle, or
at the races, and Hall-Stevenson came occasionally to visit

the Sternes. Mrs. Sterne, while she did not (naturally) approve wholly of Hall-Stevenson's way of life, found him amusing, and liked his company. She did not resent the strong friendship between the two men, as many wives might have done. However, there were times when her disapproval of the man's character overcame her amusement, and she blamed Hall-Stevenson for some of her husband's shortcomings. In one period when the master of Crazy Castle was in unusually high standing with Mrs. Sterne, the parson wrote his friend:

> She swears you are a fellow of wit, though humorous; a funny, jolly soul, though somewhat splenetic; and (bating the love of women) as honest as *gold*—how do you like the simile?

Mention of Hall-Stevenson by the diarists of the period is frequent. Most often noted was his gentlemanly manner and appearance and his excellent taste. He entertained well: his table always bore good food and fine wines. But his activities as a host, if they brought him fame, also brought him notoriety. He was the guiding spirit of the much abused Demoniacs.

The Demoniacs, who made Crazy Castle their headquarters, were probably inspired by a notorious group known as "The Monks of Medmenham Abbey." Out of the ill fame which attended the orgies of the Medmenham group, Hall-Stevenson conceived the idea for the Demoniacs. In fact, John Wilkes and Sir Francis Dashwood, leaders of the "Franciscans" of Medmenham, later were visitors at Skelton, and may have been included in the Demoniacs. Among the others of the Demoniacs were the Rev. Robert Lascelles, whom Sterne refers to in his letters as "Panty" (after Rabelais' Pantagruel); a schoolmaster, Andrew Irvine, known affectionately as "Paddy Andrew"; an architect, identified only as "Don Pringello," whose love for Crazy Castle in its pristine state prevented him from rebuilding it; Zachary Moore, whose chief occupation in life was the dissipation of a large fortune; and other merry souls, identified as a "Cardinal Scroope" and "the Colonels."

It is not difficult to picture the "orgies" which were so denounced by Sterne's Victorian commentators. The men gathered around bottles of Hall-Stevenson's good wine, talked of books and men, and indulged their fancies in fantastic, often bawdy, tales. Viewed through the Victorian mist, they were indeed sinful orgies, but from the more carnal view of the twentieth century, they are hardly shocking. Every city in the United States has convivial clubs to match the notorious Demoniacs, and the meetings of Sterne's friends were on a high moral plane when compared with the typical "conventions" of our American male "lodges" or manufacturers' associations.

But the influence of these meetings on Sterne was vastly important. Here, in an atmosphere of talkativeness, of tongues loosened by the flow of good wine, of an interchange of ideas and opinions (not always, of course, wholesome ideas and opinions), Sterne developed much of the easy conversational style and broad drollery of *Tristram Shandy*. To deplore the unwholesome influence of this association is useless; the Sterne that has come down to us is the whole Sterne; his books intermingle the good and the bad, and it is more than likely that if he had chosen to present his work in any other manner than he did, it would not have survived.

In those years when Sterne was an unknown and unimportant clergyman, he traveled often the road to Skelton. He passed often the great Grecian urn, with the sculptured owl perched upon it, standing guard over the approach to Crazy Castle, and he looked into the glassy, weed-grown waters of the ancient moat. Many times he drew his cloak more closely around him, as he felt that "pestiferous" east wind blowing over the turret, although he assured his friend that he valued "the north-east wind and all its powers not a straw." The wind, which Hall-Stevenson so dreaded, plays an amusing role in an anecdote of this period.

With the passing of years, the lord of Skelton had become a confirmed hypochondriac, and he became more and more convinced that the east wind was the cause of his various ailments. It was said that every morning when he arose he looked at the weathervane. If the instrument showed the wind in the east, he retired to his rooms and did not set foot out until the wind changed. Sterne, seeing an opportunity for a joke on his friend, paid a servant to climb up on the tower and fasten the windvane. When Hall arose in the morning, he found the wind in the opposite quarter and he came down to meet his guests in high spirits. Everything continued serene for several days, until one night when a high gust of wind tore loose the windvane and sent it pointing out the east wind. The outraged Hall retired to his chamber, and no pleading or cajoling would bring him out until the danger signal was relaxed.

But it was not all carousing and gaiety when Sterne visited Crazy Castle. He spent many quiet afternoons in the library, poring over the queer volumes in which Hall-Stevenson delighted. Perhaps it was here that he spent hours among the pages of Robert Burton's unequalled compendium of life, the *Anatomy of Melancholy,* from which he borrowed so liberally for *Tristram Shandy.*

Perhaps here he conceived the story of the traveler with the great nose, or Walter Shandy's philosophy of Christian names:

> His opinion, in this matter, was, That there was a strange kind of magic bias, which good or bad names, as he called them, irresistibly impressed upon our characters and conduct.
>
> The hero of Cervantes argued not the point with more seriousness,——nor had he more faith,——or more to say on the powers of necromancy in dishonouring his deeds,——or on Dulcinea's name, in shedding lustre upon them, than my father had on those of Trismegistus or Archimedes, on the one hand—or of Nyky and Simkin on the other. How many Caesars and Pompeys, he would say, by mere inspiration of the names, have been rendered worthy of them? And how many, he would add, are there, who might have done exceeding well in the world, had not their characters and spirits been totally depressed and Nicodemus'd into nothing?

His visits to Crazy Castle left Sterne with such pleasant memories, that we find his thoughts reverting to its ancient towers during his sojourn in France, on his visits to London, or in the weeks of lonely retirement in his parsonage. "Oh! how I envy you all at Crazy Castle," he wrote from Toulouse. "I could like to spend a month with you—and should return back again for the vintage. I honour the man who has given the world an idea of our parental seat —'tis well done. I look at it ten times a day with a *quando te aspiciam?* Now farewell—remember me to my beloved Colonel—greet Panty most lovingly on my behalf—" And again: "If I had nothing to stop me, I would engage to set out this morning, and knock at Crazy Castle gates in three days less time—by which time I should find you and the Colonel, Panty, etc., all alone—the season I most wish and like to be with you."

Much happened in the intervening years before those letters were written. Events had changed Laurence Sterne from an unknown country churchman to a great man of letters, feted in the dining rooms and salons of England and France. But the course of Sterne's life—and more especially—his literary career owed a great deal to the evenings he spent under the gloomy roofs of Skelton, with its convivial Demoniacs.

VII

The Emergence of Yorick

DESPITE Sterne's ventures in farming and his love of
conviviality, he was always a conscientious man of the
church.   He preached at Sutton and Stillington, as his
duties required, rode the rounds of his parishes and fulfilled many of the routine duties of his offices.   His sermons had attracted some attention in York, and on several
occasions he was asked to deliver special addresses.   One
of these, *The Case of Elijah and the Widow of Zarephath
Consider'd,* was preached at the annual meeting for the
benefit of two charitable foundations for York children.
His appeal was so successful—resulting in the collection of
sixty-four pounds—that the sermon was reprinted as a
pamphlet.   Appearing in 1747, it thus became the first
known publication of Sterne's writings in book form.
One other sermon preached by Sterne is known to have
been published as a pamphlet.   This was *The Abuses of
Conscience,* preached at the summer assizes in York on
July 29, 1750.   This sermon was one of Sterne's favorites,
and it is in fact an excellent sample of his best serious
writing for the church.   Ten years later, in selecting a
sermon to include in the first volumes of *Tristram Shandy*
as from the pen of Yorick, he chose this one.

But, in spite of the favor with which Sterne's service in
the church had been received, he found the road to ad-

vancement closed to him. Back of Sterne's failure to find
preferment in York is a story of dissension and intrigue in
cathedral circles worthy of a political court.

"The '45"—as the romantic but ill-advised Stuart uprising of 1745 was known—played an important part in
Sterne's life and in his future writing. The Stuarts, driven
from the British throne in 1688, had never given up hope
of reclaiming their succession, and half a century after
their exile from England they seized what appeared to be
the opportune moment. Through the circuitous route of
trade disputes with Spain and participation in the War of
the Austrian Succession, England had become involved in
an undeclared war with France. The French, seeing in
the handsome twenty-four-year-old Prince Charlie, latest
of the Stuart claimants, a chance to embarrass and divide
the British, outfitted a force of 10,000 men, under Marshal
Saxe, which set out from Dunkirk in January, 1744, to attempt an invasion of England. But the channel defense
had been carefully prepared by the English, and the
French were further hampered by a violent storm. The
result was complete failure and rout of the expedition,
and the fleet returned shattered to French haven. Soon
after, the French issued a declaration of war and King
George II eagerly took up the challenge.

But the "Bonnie Prince" had not given up. His youthful zeal and devotion led him to underestimate the difficulties of what was manifestly impossible. After the first
disastrous failure, France officially lost interest in the
Stuart cause, and Charles made arrangements to carry on
his campaign alone, aided only by his adherents in Scotland and England. For two centuries biographers, nov-
elists and historians have been intrigued by the picture
of the brave and charming young prince setting forth
alone on the desperate adventure of subduing a nation

and placing himself on its throne. He is said to have made his father as gallant a promise as ever a romantic dramatist could have written for a footlight prince: "I go, Sire, in search of three crowns, which I doubt not but to have the honor and happiness of laying at your Majesty's feet. If I fail in the attempt your next sight of me shall be in my coffin."

The English had suffered severe defeats on the Continent, and Charles chose his moment with care. He set out from France with only seven followers, and on July 25, 1745, he landed on the coast of Scotland to attempt the conquest of the British Isles! The recklessness and foolhardiness of his adventure are apparent at this distance, yet he came closer to success than seems possible. Many of the highland clans, fierce in family pride and almost barbaric in their zeal for battle, came to his assistance, and some of his Jacobite followers from England supplied money and men to his cause. The British Government found it rather hard, in fact, to arouse great popular feeling against the young prince, and resorted to placards and propaganda describing the invaders as "Papists" supported by barbarians.

Prince Charlie found quick success in the North, winning several modest victories and occupying the capital city of Edinburgh just fifty-four days after his landing. By the end of September he was ready to undertake the invasion of England, but he halted for a month of preparation, and it was the last day of October before he finally set his columns toward London. He managed, by evading the main armies of the Crown, to get as far as Derby, only a little more than a hundred miles from London. Here his Scottish chieftains, foreseeing certain defeat, persuaded him to turn back, and a dismal retreat was started back into the highlands. The armies of the Prince spent a terrible winter in the hills, and by April, when the Duke of Cumberland marched forward with 9,000 well trained and well equipped troops to join the issue, Charles had no more than 5,000 ragged, half-starved men with whom to offer battle.

Of the result there could be no doubt. The armies of Prince Charlie were routed and cut down mercilessly, and Cumberland carried on his campaign of annihilation of the Stuart followers so ruthlessly that he earned the popular title of "the butcher." The "Bonnie Prince" escaped and remained in hiding at various places on the Scottish coast for five months, with a price of 30,000 pounds sterling on his head. In the autumn of 1745 he returned to France, and he spent the remaining forty-two years of his life in dissipation and bitter frustration.

"The '45" left in its wake the bitterness and hatreds that only a deep-rooted civil war can bring forth. Not only were political issues involved, but issues of nationality and religion as well. The first Hanover king, George I, had come to England in 1714, bringing with him his thirty-one-year-old son, who became George II in 1727. Throughout the War of the Austrian Succession and the war with France, the interests of the King were more concerned with Hanover than with England, much to the resentment of large groups of Englishmen. There was widespread feeling that England's national interests were being sacrificed to the minor interests of a little German Electorate. Even greater was the religious tension prevalent through "the '45." Because the Stuart cause had French and Catholic support, the Stuart followers were indiscriminately classed as "Papists," and anti-Catholic feeling ran high. This fact was to exercise a considerable influence over the elements that led Sterne to produce *Tristram Shandy*.

After the Hanovers had succeeded in quelling the disturbances of 1745, there appeared in York a cleavage in the cathedral ranks. Led by the Archbishop, at that time Matthew Hutton, were the older prelates, conservatives in politics as well as religion. On the other side were the younger men, the liberals, whose leader was Dean Fountayne, who had been a companion of Sterne at Cambridge. Sterne's uncle Jaques, who was now his direct superior as Archdeacon of Cleveland, joined forces with the Archbishop, no doubt seeing in this alignment an opportunity to add new offices to a list already long enough to account for an income of nine hundred pounds a year. Laurence, on the other hand, aligned himself with Dean Fountayne, and rebelled against his uncle's domination.

An inkling as to the beginnings of the breach between uncle and nephew is given in the memoir to Lydia:

> —he quarreled with me afterwards because I would not write paragraphs in the newspapers:—though he was a party-man, I was not, and detested such dirty work: thinking it beneath me. From that period he became my bitterest enemy.—

That this prostitution of his nephew's talents by the uncle lay directly behind their quarrel is further borne out by a letter he wrote to a friend just before the publication of *Tristram Shandy:* "Now for your desire of knowing the reason of my turning author? why truly I am tired of employing my brains for other people's advantage.— 'Tis a foolish sacrifice I have made for some years to an ungrateful person.—"

However, there was more to the breach than a mere question of party paragraphs. Sterne had undoubtedly paid for his uncle's aid by writing such paragraphs for the local newspaper during the decade preceding their quarrel. And there is little reason to doubt that he would have

gone on writing party propaganda had he been in accord
with his uncle's view. It was not the game Sterne detested, but the side he was forced to take. Here was the
first manifestation of the turn which Sterne's character
was taking. He was ready now to assert his independence,
even against his powerful uncle and the Archbishop.

The first open outbreak of hostilities came in the autumn of 1750. For several years Sterne had been able to
increase his income considerably by preaching in York for
his colleagues who found it inconvenient to take their
turns in the cathedral. In one year this source of income
had netted him twenty pounds, and it was at this source
that Jaques struck his first blow.

The arrangements for securing substitute prebendaries
were often intrusted to John Hildyard, a York bookseller.
One autumn day Sterne entered Hildyard's shop to arrange for a sermon in the turn of Francis Blackburne, who
had by then succeeded Jaques as Archdeacon of Cleveland.
But the wily uncle had already unfurled the banner and
sounded his bugle. He had been on more or less aloof
terms with his nephew for two or three years, but now he
brought the battle into the open by letting it be known
that any favor to his nephew would be considered as an
affront to him. Inasmuch as Jaques was now Precentor
of York Cathedral, his desires were of paramount importance. As Sterne had anticipated, Blackburne had asked
Hildyard to secure a substitute speaker for him, but had
frankly intimated that Jaques might be offended if the
services of his nephew were secured.

When Sterne entered Hildyard's shop, the bookseller
took him into an inner room.

"Sir," he began uncomfortably, "my friend the Archdeacon of Cleveland not caring to preach in his turn, as I
conjectured, has left me to provide a preacher. But be-

fore I can take any steps in it with regard to you—I want first to know, sir, upon what footing you and Dr. Sterne are?"

"Upon what footing!" Sterne exclaimed.

"Yes, sir, how your quarrel stands."

The clergyman became indignant and answered heatedly, "How our quarrel stands! What's that to you? What's that to you, you puppy?"

"But, sir," Hildyard explained, "Mr. Blackburne would know."

"What's that to him?"

"But, sir, don't be angry. I only want to know of you, whether Dr. Sterne will not be displeased in case you should preach."

Sterne had that very day preached a substitute sermon. "Go look," he told the bookseller. "I've just now been preaching and you could not have fitter opportunity to be satisfied."

Hildyard attempted to mollify Sterne. "I hope, Mr. Sterne, you are not angry."

"Yes I am," Sterne answered, "but much more astonished at your impudence."

At that moment the door opened and William Herring, Chancellor of the York diocese, entered the shop. Hildyard took him aside and explained the embarrassing situation to him. The Chancellor, however, approved of Sterne as a substitute for the Archdeacon, and Hildyard returned contrite for his "impudence" to offer him the turn. In a letter to Blackburne recounting the incident, Sterne borrowed a quotation from Shakespeare to describe his feelings:

". . . . All smarting with my wounds
To be thus pestered by a Popinjay,
Out of my Grief and my Impatience

Answered neglectingly, I know not what
. . . . for he made me mad
To see him shine so bright and smell so sweet
And talk so like a waiting Gentlewoman—"

"But," the letter continues, "as I was too angry to have
the perfect faculty of recollecting poetry, however pat to
my case, so I was forced to tell him in plain prose tho'
somewhat elevated—That I would not preach, and that he
might get a parson where he could find one."

He added a postscript to the long and heated letter,
begging the Archdeacon not to let Mr. Hildyard "feel the
effects" of it. However, within the week he repented of
his hot-headedness, and addressed another letter to Blackburne apologizing for his bitterness against the bookseller,
and offering to preach the turn—which he did.

Jaques, angered because Blackburne had allowed his
nephew to preach the turn in disregard of his wishes, addressed a letter to the Archdeacon. The letter well illustrates the pernicious persecution to which Sterne was
subjected at the hands of his uncle:

> Good Mr. Archdeacon:—I will beg leave to rely upon
> your pardon for taking the liberty I do with you in
> relation to your turns of preaching in the minster.
> What occasions it is, Mr. Hildyard's employing the
> last time the only person unacceptable to me in the
> whole church, an ungrateful and unworthy nephew
> of my own, the Vicar of Sutton; and I should be
> much obliged to you, if you would please either to
> appoint any person yourself, or leave it to your Regis-
> ter to appoint one when you are not here. If any of
> my turns would suit you better than your own, I
> would change with you.

Yet, despite the strength of his uncle and the fact that
Archbishop Hutton stood with the Precentor in the quarrel, Sterne managed to keep his head above water and

might even have defeated his uncle's purpose. Through the friendship of Dean Fountayne and Lord Fauconberg, he was appointed to two minor offices, each carrying a small stipend. However, there fell into the hands of the Precentor a weapon which could hardly fail to ruin his nephew, and the vicious Jaques did not hesitate to use it. He used it, in fact, so well that Sterne was forced to wait ten years for the church preferment he desired; he used it so well that it survived Sterne's denials, found its way into common belief, was accepted throughout Sterne's life and was used in condemnation of his character after his death. Jaques' weapon was the unfounded charge that Sterne had neglected his poor mother and left her to the horrors of a debtors' prison. Everything conspired to make this the perfect standard for Jaques' campaign.

Following the death of Roger Sterne, his wife had been granted a pension of twenty pounds a year. She kept an embroidery school in Ireland, where she had settled with her one remaining daughter Catherine; and from these two sources she had an income quite sufficient to supply the modest wants of two women. For eleven years Sterne seldom heard from his mother, for in that time he was not in a position to aid her financially. However, as soon as the news of her son's marriage reached the mother, she determined to come to England, to share in what she believed to be a "fortune"—Elizabeth Lumley's income.

When Sterne heard of her arrival in England, in 1742, he took the only course open to him. He went to Liverpool to meet her and try to persuade her to return to Ireland. He could not have brought his mother and sister to live in the parsonage with his wife. The son reasoned with his mother, proving to her that the supposed "fortune" was nothing more than a small income. He gave her money and gifts, but he could not dissuade her from her course. She did, however, agree not to come to Sutton, but remain with her daughter in Chester. Sterne returned to Sutton satisfied that he had made the best of a bad situation.

But the woman who had determined to "live the rest of her days at ease" would not be satisfied with a reasonable solution. She sent Catherine to Sutton, on the pretext of paying a visit to Laurence, but actually to lay before Jaques a distorted version of the case. Catherine came in 1744, remained a month at Sterne's expense, and succeeded in poisoning her uncle's mind against her brother.

Sterne was more than fair in his attempts to arrive at a solution. He offered to set his sister up in business as a mantua maker, and furnish money for her support until her business grew sufficiently large to keep her; Mrs. Sterne offered to secure a position for Catherine in a London milliner's shop, or to recommend her for a place with a family of nobility, but Catherine refused all these offers, insisting that "as she was the daughter of a gentleman, she would not disgrace herself, but would live as such."

In spite of the unreasonableness of the attitude of his mother and sister, Sterne continued to aid them, and the total amount he gave them in cash and gifts during this period of several years was about ninety pounds, a considerable amount, considering that Sterne's income was not overly large for his needs. But his mother denied having received the money, until Sterne was forced to trace the drafts by which the money was sent. On one occasion Mrs. Sterne went to Jaques to complain against her son's treatment, but she did not tell her brother-in-law that she was carrying ten pounds with her that Laurence had given her only two days before. The embattled son offered to give his mother eight pounds a year, but she refused to accept it (perhaps with the advice of the clever Jaques) unless the amount should be settled upon her.

All of these facts Sterne urged in his own defense, when he was forced to it by his uncle's unjust persecution. Yet it is an indication of the man's character that he suffered the injustices heaped upon him by a sharp uncle and an ill-bred mother in silence, until the outrage of their accusations passed all human endurance. How or why remains a mystery, but suddenly we find the mother committed to a debtors' prison. What had happened to her pension and to the money sent her by her son has never been explained, and there is evidence that Jaques had more than a little to do with sending the woman to prison, the better to condemn his nephew for it. A fund was raised and Mrs. Sterne was released, but not until her son had suffered a final blow to his hopes for preferment. In later years a reconciliation was effected between them and she accepted the aid he had offered.

Two more factors must be noted before the incident is dismissed, and both of them are surely in Sterne's favor. The first is the fact that Mrs. Sterne had another son by a former marriage, to whom she could just as easily have turned for support; the second is the fact that Jaques could easily have helped the poor woman, if his only interest in the case had been an impersonal desire to see justice done. But, far from aiding his sister-in-law, he may have been instrumental in her imprisonment. Upon his death he left all his fortune to his housekeeper, conveniently forgetting his nephew's troubles.

So, difficult as it may be to condone Sterne's seeming coldness toward his mother, the facts clearly show that justice and truth were on the side of the son. The situation reached a climax in 1751, when Mrs. Sterne had been committed to the prison. All efforts at reconciliation with his uncle having failed, Sterne wrote a long letter to Jaques, setting forth in detail the facts in the case. Jaques refused even to be reasonable, and remained at swords' points with his nephew until the Precentor's death in 1759. He died as he lived—a disgruntled, ambitious, greedy old man. And even after his death, he still had the last thrust, in his will.

How seriously Sterne's reputation was damaged by this incident is shown in the fact that eight years after his death a letter from a Yorkshire vicar repeated the York "scandal" that "Sterne, when possessed of preferment of 300 pounds a year, would not pay ten pounds to release his mother out of Ousebridge prison, when poverty was her only fault. . . . Yet this was the man whose fine feelings gave the world the story of Le Fever and the *Sentimental Journey*. Do you not feel that something hurt you more than a cut across your finger at reading this? Talking on benevolence, or writing about it, in the most pathetic manner, and doing all the good you can without shew and parade, are very different things." The scandal followed Sterne through life, and after he became famous Walpole coined a phrase which Byron later repeated—that the author of *Tristram Shandy* would rather whine over a dead ass than relieve a living mother. How unfair the quip was need no longer be questioned.

Through the heat of his fight with Jaques and his defense of himself in his mother's case, we can see something of the weight that descended on the parson. Sterne was a man of more than normal sensitivity. He felt himself crushed by the insidiousness of the charge against him, a charge he could not publicly deny without bringing even greater injustices upon him and upon those he loved.

Out of the bitterness of these quarrels and recriminations emerged a new and changed character—the beginnings of Yorick, the bitter jester.

It is significant that so deeply was the bitterness etched into his soul that in describing Yorick, Sterne forgot he had ever been anything else. He forgot that at twenty-six this bitterness had not yet permeated his being, and Sterne's biographers have also overlooked the significance of the changes that came over the man. Sterne began to feel now that he had been cheated, hounded by the fates and the injustice of those nearest him. He saw the preferment which was his only hope in the church pass irretrievably out of his grasp, through what he felt, quite justly, was no fault of his own. The events of the next years confirmed his bitter and cynical attitude, and it was in this mood that he wrote the first installment of *Tristram Shandy,* and created for himself the role of Yorick. His characterization of Yorick is not a masterpiece of self-analysis; it could hardly be that, for Sterne felt deeply the "slings and arrows of outrageous fortune." He wrote with a pen dipped in the passionate springs of his self-pity. But if it is not an excellent analysis of the man as the world saw him, it is an excellent statement of his case against the world, dictated by his passions:

> This is all that ever staggered my faith in regard to Yorick's extraction, who, by what I can remember of him, and by all the accounts I could ever get of him, seemed not to have had one single drop of Danish blood in his whole crasis; in nine hundred years, it might possibly have all run out:——I will not philosophize one moment with you about it; for happen how it would, the fact was this:—That instead of that cold phlegm and exact regularity of sense and humors, you would have looked for, in one so extracted;—he was, on the contrary, as mercurial and

sublimated a composition,—as heteroclite a creature in all his declensions;—with as much life and whim, and *gaité de coeur* about him, as the kindliest climate could have engendered and put together. With all this sail, poor Yorick carried not one ounce of ballast; he was utterly unpracticed in the world; and, at the age of twenty-six, knew just about as well how to steer his course in it, as a romping, unsuspicious girl of thirteen: So that upon his first setting out, the brisk gale of his spirits, as you will imagine, ran him foul ten times in a day of somebody's tackling; and as the grave and more slow-paced were oftenest in his way,——you may likewise imagine, 'twas with such he had generally the ill luck to get the most entangled. For aught I know there might be some mixture of unlucky wit at the bottom of such Fracas:——For, to speak the truth, Yorick had an invincible dislike and opposition in his nature to gravity;—not to gravity as such;—for where gravity was wanted, he would be the most grave or serious of mortal men for days and weeks together;—but he was an enemy to the affectation of it, and declared open war against it, only as it appeared a cloak for ignorance, or for folly: and then, whenever it fell in his way, however sheltered and protected, he seldom gave it much quarter.

Sometimes, in his wild way of talking, he would say, that Gravity was an errant scoundrel, and he would add,—of the most dangerous kind too,—because a sly one; and that he verily believed, more honest, well-meaning people were bubbled out of their goods and money by it in one twelve-month, than by pocket-picking and shop-lifting in seven. In the naked temper which a merry heart discovered, he would say there was no danger,—but to itself.—whereas the very essence of gravity was design, and consequently deceit;—'twas a taught trick to gain credit of the world for more sense and knowledge than a man was worth; and that, with all its pretensions,—it was no better, but often worse, than what a French wit had long ago defined it,—viz. "A mysterious carriage of the

body to cover the defects of the mind";—which definition of gravity, Yorick, with great imprudence, would
say, deserved to be wrote in letters of gold.

But, in plain truth, he was a man unhackneyed
and unpractised in the world, and was altogether as
indiscreet and foolish on every subject of discourse
where policy is wont to impress restraint. Yorick had
no impression but one, and that was what arose from
the nature of the deed spoken of; which impression
he would usually translate into plain English without any periphrasis;—and too oft without much dis-
tinction of either person, time, or place;—so that
when mention was made of a pitiful or an ungenerous proceeding——he never gave himself a moment's
time to reflect who was the hero of the piece,——what
his station,——or how far he had power to hurt him
hereafter;——but if it was a dirty action,—without
more ado,—The man was a dirty fellow,—and so on.—
And as his comments had usually the ill fate to be
terminated either in a *bon mot,* or to be enlivened
throughout with some drollery or humor of expression, it gave wings to Yorick's indiscretion. In a
word, tho' he never sought, yet, at the same time, as
he seldom shunned occasions of saying what came
uppermost, and without much ceremony:——he had
but too many temptations in life, of scattering his wit
and his humour,—his gibes and his jests about him.
——They were not lost for want of gathering.

Against this indiscretion of his, Yorick is warned by John
Hall-Stevenson, in the guise of Eugenius (certainly Hall
is the last person one expects to see cast in the role of
counsellor to the indiscreet!). And we find the tragic
story of Sterne's family quarrels re-enacted in the book,
somewhat embellished by a justified self-pity:

Eugenius . . . would often tell him, that one day or
other he would certainly be reckoned with; and he
would often add, in an accent of sorrowful apprehension,—to the uttermost mite. . . .

Trust me, dear Yorick, this unwary pleasantry of thine will sooner or later bring thee into scrapes and difficulties, which no after-wit can extricate thee out of.——In these sallies, too oft, I see, it happens, that a person laughed at, considers himself in the light of a person injured, with all the rights of such a situation belonging to him; and when thou viewest him in that light too, and reckons up his friends, his family, his kindred and allies,——and musters up with them the many recruits which will list under him from a sense of common danger;——'tis no extravagant arithmetic to say, that for every ten jokes,—thou hast got an hundred enemies.

. . . . .

Revenge from some baneful corner shall level a tale of dishonour at thee, which no innocence of heart or integrity of conduct shall set right.——The fortunes of thy house shall totter,—thy character, which led the way to them, shall bleed on every side of it,—thy faith questioned,—thy works belied,—thy wit forgotten,—thy learning trampled on. . . .——trust me, Yorick, when to gratify a private appetite, it is once resolved upon, that an innocent and an helpless creature shall be sacrificed, 'tis an easy matter to pick up sticks enough from any thicket where it has strayed, to make a fire to offer it up with.

Yorick resolved to be more cautious, but too late—his enemies had already formed against him, and his past indiscretions came crashing down upon him:

—The whole plan of attack, just as Eugenius had fore-boded, was put in execution all at once,—with so little mercy on the side of the allies,—and so little suspicion in Yorick, of what was carrying on against him, —that when he thought, good easy man! full surely preferment was o' ripening,—they had smote his root, and then he fell, as many a worthy man had fallen before him.

Yorick, however, fought it out with all imaginable

gallantry for some time; till, overpowered by numbers, and worn out at length by the calamities of the war,—but more so, by the ungenerous manner in which it was carried on,—he threw down the sword; and though he kept up his spirits in appearance to the last, he died, nevertheless, as was generally thought, quite broken-hearted.

It need hardly be pointed out that Sterne did not die, like Yorick, under the blows of his enemies. But how his sensitive soul must have suffered, to have retained such a bitter memory for ten years, until the time when he set it down on paper for the world to read. The Sterne that survived was a different Sterne. He was no longer the youthful, easy going parson, with a quip and a jest to shock the staid. Beside Sterne the jester, appeared a character that could give fuller meaning to the term *sentimental*, which he had adopted. Here was a man who had suffered, and had sympathy for the oppressed. Here was a rebel against the conventionally smug and the haughtily stupid. Never did his feeling and his rebellion find full expression, for they had to be tempered with a jest, to keep his public amused. But occasionally there are glimpses of true feeling—as in his plea for the Negro slaves, or when he thought of the Inquisition. And occasionally the rebel came to the fore—in his fierce attacks on the pretense of the medical profession, in his frank admission that he fled Paris out of disgust at the hypocrisy of French etiquette. Here was the significant flowering of that side of Sterne's character too long overlooked by his biographers. Here was the beginning of the Sterne who could dip his pen in vitriol and write *Tristram Shandy;* here began the man whose feelings enabled him to draw his tender portraits, his sympathetic sketches. The events of these years shaped the pattern of Sterne's career. Without them, his writings might have remained to the end as admirable as his sermons or his verse on the unknown world of death—as admirable and as unimportant.

Out of the bitterness of these years emerged also a full-blown philosophy of life. It was a hedonism of a sort: Yorick learned to live his life keenly, with a zest for whatever pleasure the day might bring. So well did he practice this philosophy that a decade later a journalist in Paris was struck by Sterne's ability to take from life the fullest measure of enjoyment.

VIII

"Dear, Dear Kitty"

LITTLE is known of the events of the next few years.
Externally, little of importance came to the vicar of Sutton.
His farming experiments having proved a dismal failure,
he began to extricate himself from his land entanglements.
By 1758, he was able to write to his friend, John Blake of
York:

> I thank God, however, I have settled most of my
> affairs—let my freehold to a promising tenant—have
> likewise this week let him the most considerable part
> of my tyths, and shall clear my hands and head of all
> county entanglements, having at present only ten
> pounds a year in land and seven pounds a year in
> Corn Tyth left undisposed of, which shall be quitted
> with all prudent speed. This will bring me and mine
> into a narrow compass, and make us, I hope, both
> rich and happy. 'Tis only to friends we thus un-
> bosome ourselves—

Occasionally Mr. and Mrs. Sterne would ride into York
to visit Blake, who was also a clergyman. Although the
friendship lasted for many years, it appears to have been
one of those amiable family friendships, more admirable
from a moral and domestic point of view than the companionship of Hall-Stevenson; but from the literary point
of view, of little importance. We find Sterne interesting

himself in Blake's affairs of the heart, offering him sound advice on the wiles of women; he reports on the condi- tion of his Lydia's asthma, and fears she is "somewhat relapsing"; he sends "a large Quantity of Pepiermint which I beg you will disstil carefully for me." The friend- ship, however, offers a glimpse of another facet of Sterne's paradoxical character, for here he is always amiable and considerate. As far as the records show, the storm clouds that hovered over Sterne never darkened this pleasant association.

The most important days of this period, however, were those which Sterne spent in his study and in the library at Skelton. Although it is quite unlikely that Sterne anticipated a career in literature, nevertheless *Tristram Shandy* was already gestating in his brain. The "homun- culus" injected by the fire of his quarrel with Jaques was feeding on the rich store of literary curios in Hall-Steven- son's library and his own study. Now, in addition to his readings in the humorists, he began to delve into the books on military theory. The introduction of gun- powder as a lethal medium had altered the entire science of military tactics, and Sterne, with a curious whimsy, found much humor—albeit unintentional—in the absurdly pompous treatises of the militarists. They were the apos- tles of a new order, summed up briefly by Toby—". . . we read over the siege of Troy which lasted ten years and eight months,—though with such a train of artillery as we had at Namur, the town might have been carried in a week—"

During this decade of the 1750's, the vicar of Sutton appears to have published nothing. A manuscript was examined by the late M. Paul Stapfer, Sterne's French biographer, which has been attributed to this period. This is a reflection on the complexity of the universe, and

man's relative unimportance. Walking into his orchard
one night, the philosopher came upon a plum tree. The
plums hung in clusters, like stars in the constellations,
and some the wind had blown to the ground. Each little
plum became to him suddenly a world in itself, with its
myriads of tiny beings, its armies of conquest, its hopes
and ambitions. He philosophized:

> O the vanity of worldly things, and even of worlds
> themselves! O world, wherein I have spent so many
> happy days! O the comforts, and enjoyments I am
> separated from; the acquaintance and friends I have
> left behind me there! O the mountains, rivers, rocks,
> and plains, which ages had familiariz'd to my view!
> with you I seemed at home; here I am like a ban-
> ished man; everything appears strange, wild and sav-
> age! O the projects I had form'd! the designs I had
> set on foot, the friendships I had cultivated! How
> has one blast of wind dash'd you to pieces.
>
> . . . .
>
> "And now a Bubble burst, and now a world." The
> time will come when the powers of heaven shall be
> shaken, and the stars shall fall like the fruit of a tree,
> when it is shaken by a mighty wind!

The thought was suggested by a work widely read at
the time—Fontenelle's essay on the plurality of worlds.
That he had read and been influenced by Pope's *Essay on
Man* is also apparent from the fact that he chose a quotation from Pope to summarize his thought. The philosophy and style are conventional enough, and the entire
performance shows that Sterne was not yet ready to give
the world a literary masterpiece. At best this was merely
an imitative essay in composition. But it does indicate
that Sterne sometimes sought escape from reality in the
world of words. If he was not yet ready to write, at least
the germ was doing its work within him, and uncon-

sciously he was groping toward his *forte*. And it was a quarrel again which brought the matter to a climax, and directly led the way to *Tristram Shandy*.

The quarrel burst upon the public view in 1758, but the beginnings go back several years. Prominent in cathedral intrigues was a church lawyer, Dr. Francis Topham of York. This Topham was characterized by Sterne as a "little, dirty, pimping, pettifogging, ambidextrous fellow, who neither cared what he did or said of anyone, provided he could get a penny by it." He was, like Gilbert and Sullivan's Pooh-Bah, an amazing pluralist. Pooh-Bah was "First Lord of the Treasury, Lord Chief Justice, Commander-in-Chief, Lord High Admiral, Master of the Buck Hounds, Groom of the Back Stairs, Archbishop of Titipu, and Lord Mayor, both acting and elect." "Did I not," he asks, "unhesitatingly accept all their posts at once?" "And the salaries attached to them?" Pish-Tush reminds him. "You did." Impressive as was Pooh-Bah's list, Dr. Topham's was even more so. For he was "Master of the Faculties, Commissary to the Archbishop of York, Official to the Archdeacon of York, Official to the Archdeacon of the East Riding, Official to the Archdeacon of Cleveland, Official to the Peculiar Jurisdiction of Howdenshire, Official to the Precentor, Official to the Chancellor of the Church of York, Official to several of the Prebendaries of York Cathedral, and Commissary and Keeper-General of the Exchequer and Prerogative Courts of the Archbishop of York."

Sterne incurred the pluralist's hatred in 1751, when Dean Fountayne appointed the parson to the commissaryship of the Peculiar Court of Pickering and Pocklington. Dr. Topham, ever on the search for new offices, had expected to receive this one, the fees from which amounted to six pounds a year. Behind Sterne's appointment to it lies an interesting story. In that year Dean Fountayne was to go down to Cambridge, for his doctor's degree. However, it was necessary that he prepare a dissertation in Latin. Being unequal to the task, the Dean called on his college friend, Laurence Sterne, and Sterne wrote the sermon, *Concio ad Clerum*. It was probably out of gratitude for this important service that Fountayne defied Topham and Jaques, to give the minor office to the parson.

Topham spread around York the story that Dean Fountayne had promised him the office, as well as the commissaryship of the Dean and Chapter of York, and had broken his promise. The storm broke at a dinner of church officials. Dean Fountayne, with Sterne's support, openly accused Topham of spreading a malicious rumor, and Topham, at last forced to admit the charge, was publicly disgraced.

This disgrace rankled in the breast of the ecclesiastical Pooh-Bah. For several years he nursed a smoldering hatred of Dean Fountayne, Sterne and several other clergymen who had opposed him. But it was not until 1758 that the quarrel again burst forth. The most lucrative office held by Topham was the commissaryship of the Exchequer and Prerogative Courts, and the greedy lawyer hoped to secure this office for his son, after his own death. Again finding opposition among the Dean and chapter, and again being frustrated in his plan, Dr. Topham brought his grievances into public view. In December, 1758, he published an anonymous pamphlet entitled *A Letter Addressed to the Reverend the Dean of York; In which is given A full Detail of some very extraordinary Behaviour of his, in relation to his Denial of a Promise made by him to Dr. Topham*. The Dean, feeling that the public should be acquainted with the facts, answered this pamphlet with one entitled *An Answer to a Letter Address'd to the Dean of York, In the Name of Dr. Topham*.

The public greeted the pamphlets warmly, but not quite in the spirit Topham hoped for. York was amused at the spectacle of supposedly dignified churchmen bickering like children forth and back in anonymous pamphlets. Scandal-mongering tongues never wag so freely and so gleefully as when clergymen are the victims, and York gossips indulged in a Roman holiday. Their glee reached a peak, when Dr. Topham brought forth another heated pamphlet, which he called *A Reply to the Answer to a Letter Lately addressed to the Dean of York*. In a sarcastic vein he attacked the Dean, and suggested that Sterne had been the true author of the Dean's pamphlet (which may well have been a fact).

Now Sterne entered the battle in earnest. He wrote and had printed a pamphlet entitled *A Political Romance, Addressed to —————————, Esq; Of York*. The work is now called *The History of a Good, Warm Watch-Coat*. Sterne told the story of the quarrel in allegory, making Topham look ridiculous. He described the disputed commissaryship of Pickering and Pocklington as an old, worn-out pair of black plush breeches, and he assailed Topham's imposing list of offices in a manner of ridicule:

> . . . . are you not Sexton and Dog-Whipper, worth three pounds a year? Then you begged the church wardens to let your wife have the washing and darning of the church-linen, which brings you in thirteen shillings and four-pence:—then you have six shillings and eight-pence for oiling and winding up the clock; both paid you at Easter:—the pounder's place, which is worth forty shillings a year, you have got that too: —you are a bailiff, which the late parson got you, which brings you in forty shillings more. Besides all this, you have six pounds a year paid you quarterly, for being mole-catcher to the parish.—

The climax of the dispute—the attempt of Topham to

secure his commissaryship for his son—Sterne handled in a similar vein. The office was alluded to as a watch-coat, and "nothing would serve Trim but he must take it home, in order to have it converted into a *warm under-petticoat* for his wife, and a *jerkin* for himself against the winter."

How this recital would have pleased the citizens of York! To see the whole dispute held up in such ludicrous light would have been balm to the soul of scandal. But cool heads, fearful of the consequences, prevailed. Topham, knowing he could never find the words to answer this pamphlet, agreed to withdraw his suit on condition the booklet be suppressed. The Chancellor of the diocese, and even Dean Fountayne himself, urged Sterne not to make public his "Romance." Sterne, much against his will for he valued the forthright appraisal of a ridiculous argument more than the appearance of dignity, was at last persuaded, and all the known copies were burned. A few, however, survived, to give us the amusing story of church intrigue.

The suppression, as events proved, was a determining factor in Sterne's life, for with it came his decision to launch an essay at a writing career. The very month that saw his "Political Romance" go up in flames—January, 1759—saw the beginning of *Tristram Shandy*.

Meanwhile, Sterne's domestic affairs had become strained to the very limit of endurance. His marriage from the first was an ill-starred venture, and one doomed to certain failure. Elizabeth Lumley was not the sort of woman to hold and guide the affections of a man like Sterne—if indeed any woman could have. His temperament made it difficult for him to impose upon himself those emotional readjustments necessary for the smooth conduct of his household. Elizabeth's conventionally dull and stolid mind could not keep pace with the keen mind of her husband, and differences soon arose between them. Then, too, the trouble with Sterne's ungrateful mother and sister must have been the cause of many a domestic upheaval. It may be that Elizabeth tried also to exercise that "arm of flesh," which her cousin had attributed to her, and she was probably disappointed to find her husband a poor subject for such domination.

At any rate—whatever the causes, and there must have been many—by about 1750 the marriage had lost whatever luster it possessed, and became merely a thing to be endured. There was no open break between the Sternes, but their natural differences asserted themselves, and the breach grew ever wider. If we can accept an assertion made by Sterne many years later at its face value, they did not even share a sex-life together after about 1751 or 1752.

If Sterne's temperament was ill suited to marriage, Mrs. Sterne's was even less conducive to domestic tranquillity. She was a domineering sort of woman, with a shrill voice —on occasion the neighborhood had reason to be aware of that shrillness. Her failure to dominate her husband resulted in a retreat from reality; she fancied herself ill-used and neglected by her relatives, and at length she even turned Mrs. Montagu against her. Her frustration, the fancied insults of her family and sadness over the death of her sister at last found their mark in her mind, and she suffered a mental collapse in the summer of 1759, when Sterne was at work on his *Shandy*.

It is a tragedy of the mentally ill that their delusions assume such ludicrous patterns. Mrs. Sterne, whose instinct of domination was thwarted by life, in her illness fancied herself the Queen of Bohemia. During this period Sterne did everything to aid her. He took a house at York, in order that she might have the best medical care.

He humored her fancy, and arranged her affairs as be-fitted the Queen of such a state.

In the midst of these unhappy scenes, Sterne's embat-tled mother died. Jaques followed her in death after two months. With their deaths passed the last tie that held the parson to the Sterne line, although before his own death he remembered his sister kindly.

All of these factors bore down heavily on Sterne, and it was largely to find relief from his moods that he threw his energies into the completion of *Tristram Shandy*. Through the summer and autumn of 1759 he worked away on the first two volumes, and sometime during the summer he had the work near enough to completion to think of its publication. And it was at this time that Sterne embarked on the first of a long line of light flirta-tions for which his memory has been long damned.

In the reign of Louis XIV many Huguenots were driven from France after the revocation of the Edict of Nantes. The properties of these religious exiles were often confiscated, and they were forced to flee the country penniless. One of these exile families may have been that of Beranger de Fourmantelle. One daughter re-turned to France, became a convert to Catholicism, and received the family properties. The other daughter, Cath-erine, and her mother settled in London, where Catherine found employment as a singer. In the autumn of 1759 they left London for York, where Catherine was to sing at the winter concerts.

It was probably at one of these concerts at the Assembly Rooms that Sterne saw and was captivated by his "dear, dear Kitty." They talked, and Sterne offered to paint her portrait—he had long dabbled in paints as a hobby. She accepted his friendship eagerly, and an intimacy soon de-veloped between them. They were seen frequently on the streets of York, or in the shops; they drove together, or sat late over a bottle of good wine. Sterne, as always, was completely open in the affair, and it is an interesting commentary on the temper of the time that York found nothing wrong in the open sight of a cathedral prebendary's affair with an attractive young singer.

The flirtation may be traced through the series of short letters Sterne addressed to his "dear, dear Kitty." The first—distinguished by the somewhat formal salutation—accompanied a gift of wine:

> Miss—
> I shall be out of all humour with you, and besides *will not paint your picture in black, which best becomes you,* unless you accept a few bottles of Calcavalla which I have ordered my man will leave at the *dore* in my absence. The reason of this trifling present you shall know on Tuesday night, and I half insist upon it that you invent some plausible excuse to be home by 7.

The gift of wine, and the "reason of this trifling present" must have been quite satisfactory, for the next letter is in a much more familiar strain:

> My dear Kitty,
> I have sent you a pot of sweetmeats and a pot of Honey, neither of them half so sweet as yourself; but don't be vain upon this, or presume to grow sour upon this character of sweetness I give you; for if you do, I shall send you a pot of pickles (by way of contrarys) to sweeten you up and bring you to yourself again. Whatever changes happen to you, believe me that I am unalterably yours—

A copy of his sermon on Elijah and the widow of Zarephath went to her, and he professed to "see something of the same kind and gentle disposition in your heart which I have painted in the prophet's." Then, at the height of the flirtation, after a Saturday night's philandering, came this note, which represents Sterne in his best—or worst—mood as a lover:

> My dear Kitty,
> If this billet catches you in bed, you are a lazy, sleepy little slut, and I am a giddy, foolish, unthinking fellow for keeping you so late up; but this Sabbath is a day of sorrow—for I shall not see my dear creature, unless you meet me at Taylor's half an hour after twelve; but in this, do as you like. I have ordered Matthew to turn thief and steal you a quart of Honey. What is Honey to the sweetness of thee who are sweeter than all the flowers it comes from? I love you to distraction, Kitty, and will love you to eternity, so adieu! and believe what time only will prove me, that I am yours.

Here, in this affair, we have the first real instance of that "unfaithfulness" to his marriage vows for which Thackeray and other critics have so condemned Sterne. Yet the fact is that Sterne's marriage had long become merely a word. Whatever there had been of love in it had long gone, and Mrs. Sterne was indifferent to her husband's affairs. And in at least one sense Sterne maintained his honor as a husband throughout his life. Although he admitted frankly that he "must always have some Dulcinea" in his mind, to the last he demonstrated at least his material devotion as a husband and father in the careful provision he made, that his wife and daughter should never feel the strain of poverty. The fact that York accepted Sterne's affair with Kitty with such easy toleration indicates how harmless it was, for even in an age of wide moral latitude a churchman's open adultery would hardly have passed unnoticed.

Catherine de Fourmantelle found her way into the

pages of *Tristram Shandy*, as "my dear, dear Jenny," and
Sterne wrote a defense of himself in the first volume:

> —Nor is there anything unnatural or extravagant
> in the supposition, that my dear Jenny may be
> my friend.—Friend!—My friend.—Surely, Madam, a
> friendship between the two sexes may subsist, and be
> supported without——Fy! Mr. Shandy:——Without
> anything, Madam, but that tender and delicious sen-
> timent, which ever mixes in friendship, where there
> is a difference of sex.

Through the month of December, Sterne was busy with
the details of *Tristram Shandy's* publication. By the turn
of the year, Tristram had made his debut into the world
without fanfare, and the stage was set for the real drama
of Sterne's life.

IX

Tristram Shandy

IT IS an amazing fact that "dear, dear Kitty's" unmistakable influence on the first two volumes of *Tristram Shandy* has been largely overlooked by Sterne's critics and biographers. No one has failed to note that a large part of the volumes is taken up in bitter attacks on the Roman Catholic Church. In assigning a cause for Sterne's apparent bitterness, his biographers have pointed to the sharp feeling among English churchmen against Papists, after the attempted restoration of the Stuart pretender in 1745. No doubt this was partly the basis of his dislike. But Sterne would have needed a much more personal reason to inveigh as he did against the Church of Rome, and it is more than probable that he found his reason in Kitty de Fourmantelle.

Tristram Shandy, although never precisely biographical, is always a personal story. It is Sterne revealed in a thousand attitudes and situations. Its characters are largely borrowed out of the author's experiences, and few things found their way into its pages unless they had touched Sterne in his personal life. The story of Catherine de Fourmantelle, forced to leave her native France and find a life for herself and her mother abroad, was just the sort of thing that would play upon Sterne's sensitive nature, and arouse his indignation against the cause of her discomfiture. This was especially true as long as the subject of the affair was a pretty woman, for this was a fact aimed directly at the chink in Sterne's armor. From all accounts, the young lady was far from destitute or friendless; still her situation was far removed from the comfort of a French estate and a position in French society.

A significant fact long overlooked is that the bitterest passages against the Catholic Church are often to be found in the book in juxtaposition to references to "dear, dear Jenny." In the first volume, the eighteenth chapter is largely given over to small talk about his "dear, dear Jenny," and a few pages farther along he inserted a sharp satire on the Catholic decree regarding pre-natal baptism. And he chose as the medium for his satire the consultation of the French doctors of the Sorbonne modifying this decree. There is more than coincidence in this.

The Life and Opinions of Tristram Shandy, Gentleman has survived as a milestone in English literature for two reasons: its style and its characters. Sterne broke with the tradition of contemporary writing: his novel was no more a novel than it was an essay, or a book of philosophy, or a memoir, or a local satire after the manner of the pamphleteers. He wrote as he talked and as he thought; his book was loose and disjointed in structure, full of curious and difficult oddities in typography, arrangement, and pagination. Often he broke in upon his narrative with a long digression, a manner now popular with our "stream of consciousness" writers. Many of these curious devices and stratagems were not original with Sterne—but he made them acceptable to the reading public of his time. At any rate, they were hardly important in themselves, but were merely the swaddling clothes of a new development in writing and art—impressionism. Sterne made himself a part of the book. His thoughts, feelings, and attitudes were communicated to the reader, not through formal narrative, but in an easy conversational manner. Thousands of writers since Sterne have striven, consciously or unconsciously, to attain the style of *Tristram Shandy*.

But from the point of view of pure enjoyment, the most delightful factor in *Tristram Shandy* is its characters. Tristram himself hardly enters into the book, for he is not born until several volumes have passed, and he reaches the age of five when last heard from. The characters in which generations of readers have found delight are Walter Shandy, Toby Shandy, Trim, Dr. Slop, the Widow Wadman, Eugenius and Yorick. The men and women who people the pages of *Tristram Shandy* may be discovered to a large degree in the men and women who had passed through Sterne's life.

Walter Shandy was Sterne's thrust at that type of superknowledge that befogs itself with reason. He "had an itch, in common with all philosophers, of reasoning upon everything which happens, and accounting for it too." He is full of systems and syllogisms, of metaphysical arguments, of theories and hypotheses. When Walter Shandy went down to Cambridge to enter his son, the scholars were amazed to find a man so well versed in reasoning, without the blessing of a formal education—and here Sterne has his fun at the expense of the universities, which are supposed to have a monopoly on befogging controversy.

In direct opposition was his brother Toby. Toby was a simple soul, "who, of all things in the world, troubled his brain the least with abstruse thinking." Sterne found keen delight in picturing the two men engaged in endless conversations, the one gauging all things by reason and super-sophistry, the other with his too naive light of judgment:

Do you understand the theory of that affair? replied my father.

Not I, quoth my uncle.

—But you have some ideas, said my father, of what you talk about?—

No more than my horse, replied my uncle Toby.

Gracious heaven! cried my father, looking upwards, and clasping his two hands together——there is a worth in thy honest ignorance, brother Toby—— 'twere almost a pity to exchange it for a knowledge. —But I'll tell thee.—

And Walter Shandy proceeds to his long explanations, proving his point by rule and example. But my uncle Toby sits smoking his pipe, and if the conversation becomes too abstruse, he relieves himself by whistling the *Lillibullero*, or breaking in upon his long-winded brother with an honest "You puzzle me to death!" There is method in even the paradoxes of Sterne's writing, and it is significant that, although Toby had been a soldier, living the rough life of the army camps, he combined in him all the best qualities of modesty and kindliness:

My uncle Toby Shandy, Madam, was a gentleman, who, with the virtues which usually constitute the character of a man of honour and rectitude,—possessed one in a very eminent degree, which is seldom or never put into the catalogue; and that was a most extreme and unparalleled modesty of nature. . . . Whichever way my uncle Toby came by it, 'twas nevertheless modesty in the truest sense of it; and that is, Madam, not in regard to words, for he was so unhappy as to have very little choice in them—but to things;—and this kind of modesty so possessed him, and it arose to such a height in him, as almost to equal, if such a thing could be, even the modesty of a woman.

My uncle Toby was a man patient of injuries;—not

from want of courage,—I have told you in a former
chapter, "that he was a man of courage":——And will
add here, that where just occasions presented, or
called it forth,—I know no man under whose arm I
would sooner have taken shelter. . . .—but he was of a
peaceful, placid nature,—no jarring element in it,—
all was mixed up so kindly within him; my uncle
Toby had scarce a heart to retaliate upon a fly.

—Go—says he, one day at dinner, to an overgrown
one which had buzzed about his nose, and tormented
him cruelly all dinner-time,—and which after infinite
attempts, he had caught at last, as it flew by him;——
I'll not hurt thee, says my uncle Toby, rising from
his chair, and going across the room, with the fly in
his hand,——I'll not hurt a hair of thy head:—Go,
says he, lifting up the sash, and opening his hand as
he spoke, to let it escape;—go, poor devil, get thee
gone, why should I hurt thee?—This world surely is
wide enough to hold both thee and me.

Sterne's critics have too long supposed that my uncle
Toby was no more than Sterne painted him—a simple,
honest man representing all the good, sweet qualities of
humanity. Such an interpretation is so contrary to the
entire purpose and style of the book that it is a wonder
it could seriously have been proposed. There is as much
purpose and meaning in my uncle Toby as in Walter
Shandy, or Dr. Slop, or Yorick. Through the naive Toby,
who had killed men when "duty" called, but would not
harm a fly, Sterne was having his thrust at the military
theorists. For Toby had his "hobby-horse." On a bowl-
ing green he set up replicas of Dunkirk and other cities
under siege by the armies of the crown, and with minia-
ture artillery he reproduced the movements of the troops.
So far had my uncle Toby fallen under the sway of his
"hobby-horse" that no word could be spoken to him without arousing in him military thoughts:

Now, whether we observe it or no, continued my father, in every sound man's head, there is a regular succession of ideas of one sort or other, which follow each other in train just like——A train of artillery? said my uncle Toby——A train of a fiddle-stick!—— quoth my father.

Nowhere is Sterne's satire so deliciously subtle as in this instance: using Toby's naïveté to express the pompous befuddlements with which the militarists have always shrouded mass murder is sheer genius. In one paragraph Sterne himself expressed the perfection of the satire:

My father would often say to Yorick, that if any mortal in the whole universe had done such a thing, except his brother Toby, it would have been looked upon by the world as one of the most refined satires upon the parade and prancing manner in which Lewis XIV. from the beginning of the war, but particularly that very year, had taken the field—But 'tis not my brother Toby's nature, kind soul! my father would add, to insult any one.

—But let us go on.

and in one place Sterne arises in outright denunciation of the military:

—The act of killing and destroying a man, continued my father, raising his voice—and turning to my uncle Toby—you see, is glorious—and the weapons by which we do it are honourable.—We march with them upon our shoulders—We strut with them by our sides—We gild them—We carve them—We in-lay them—We enrich them—Nay, if it be but a scoundrel cannon, we cast an ornament upon the breach of it.—

In Toby's "Justifications of his own principles and conduct in wishing to continue the war," Sterne wrote the perfect epitome of absurdity of all military philosophers who attempt to show by humanistic reasoning that war is necessary or desirable.

Trim, Toby's servant, was a simple, honest corporal who, from close association with his master, had taken on many of the older man's naive qualities. It was through Trim that Sterne introduced Yorick's sermon on *The Abuses of Conscience.*

Of the little company that listened to Trim's reading of the sermon, one was ill at ease. This was Dr. Slop, the bitterest portrait in Sterne's gallery. Many factors combined to produce Dr. Slop, a horrible effigy of the medical profession and Catholicism.

It has long been accepted that the original of Dr. Slop was Dr. John Burton of York. Burton, who had gained some attention in medical circles with books and treatises on the new science of obstetrics, was well known in York as a physician and philanthropist. But he was suspected of being a Papist and a Stuart sympathizer, and during the chaos surrounding the uprising of 1745, Jaques Sterne had the physician arrested and thrown into prison. Sterne's dislike of the "man-midwife" has long been traced to this, but it appears much more likely that Sterne had more personal grievances against him. The fact that Burton was a Papist, when linked to Kitty de Fourmantelle's treatment at the hands of Catholics, serves as a clue. If the full story of the birth and death of the first little Lydia were known, perhaps it would offer another clue to Sterne's hatred of the "man-midwife" and indeed the whole science of "man-midwifery." Finally, we need only look at Sterne's life-long illness, with its corollary of distrust of the medical profession, to find the final link in the chain of circumstances which resulted in Dr. Slop:

> Imagine to yourself a little squat, uncourtly figure
> of a Dr. Slop, of about four feet and a half perpen-

dicular height, with a breadth of back, and a sesqui-
pedality of belly, which might have done honour to
a serjeant in the horse-guards.

This is the reader's introduction to the character who
was to be the butt of Sterne's thrusts against Catholicism
and the medical profession. In many instances this hatred
of Popery mars the early volumes of *Tristram Shandy;*
however, Sterne was not one to hold forever such an un-
worthy prejudice—following his visits to France, where he
lived amicably among Catholics, his attacks on them
ceased. It is interesting to note, nevertheless, that this
was long after the plight of Kitty de Fourmantelle had
ceased to trouble him. His hatred of the medical bigwigs
never left him, and he continued to the end—not without
justification, as will be seen—to curse them as blunderers
and charlatans.

Dr. Slop was the "man-midwife" who, by his blunders in
his attendance upon Mrs. Shandy, brought forth little
Tristram with a crushed nose, thus opening the way for
a long dissertation by Walter Shandy on noses. There is
much humor in Sterne's treatment of the incident, but it
is humor with a sharp barb. There is no doubt that he
intensely disliked the "man-midwife." (Can it be the first
little Lydia suffered at the hands of a blundering doctor?)

Many of the other characters in the book have been
already mentioned in these pages. Dear, dear Jenny, who
could be only Kitty de Fourmantelle; Eugenius, the sage
friend of Yorick, who was admittedly John Hall-Stevenson; Yorick, who was Sterne himself. To these we can
add Didius, the church lawyer, who was an obvious paper
counterpart of Topham, Sterne's antagonist in the commissaryship of Pickering and Pocklington; and numerous
others, who were taken from the streets of York and thrust
bodily into the book.

From this it becomes evident that Sterne's major intention in writing the first two volumes of *Tristram Shandy* was to write a local satire on York affairs. The characters were so thinly disguised as to be readily recognizable to Yorkshire citizens, and there are frequent allusions to local events. The word *Shandy*, in fact, was a Yorkshire colloquialism, used to describe persons who were odd—who, to use an Americanism much in vogue recently, were *pixillated*. Sterne may have hoped for a wider audience, but he did not expect too much; it is certain he never dreamed of the sort of reception his book actually had.

To the extent already noted *Tristram Shandy* was autobiographical; Sterne undoubtedly hoped to find vindication in some quarters, revenge in others, through its publication. However, it cannot be stressed too much that the autobiographical elements are to be found in the characterizations, thoughts, and attitudes expressed, rather than in the details of events in the book. Many of Sterne's critics and biographers have been misled in attempting to read into the incidents of the book a too literal narrative of the events of the author's life.

With the first two volumes completed in the late autumn of 1759, Sterne set about to publish the work. He had worked on his book through the summer, but he evidently made changes practically up to the minute of its going to press. The references to "dear, dear Jenny" and much of the anti-Papist material were late insertions, and the sermon was undoubtedly an after-thought, to strengthen his attacks on Popery (and perhaps to open the way for the sale of a volume of sermons).

As early as the summer of 1759, Sterne had already sounded out the publishing firm of Dodsley in London, after having offered the volumes to local booksellers. Dodsley refused to handle the work, declaring that its success was too doubtful for his firm to venture upon it. Sterne then proceeded to edit his work, pruning away much of it that might have been too offensive, and adding new material. Many of Sterne's friends professed an interest in the book, and one offered the author a hundred pounds toward the cost of publication. With the printing costs thus defrayed, Sterne determined to bring the books out himself, and by late November all arrangements had been made. The volumes were to be placed on sale in the shop of John Hinxman, who had succeeded Hildyard as York's leading bookseller. Sterne had written again to Dodsley, informing him that the volumes were to be printed, and asking the publisher's aid in the sale:

> If my book sells and has the run our critics expect, I propose to free myself of all future troubles of the kind (*i.e.,* of printing), and bargain with you, if possible, for the rest as they come out, which will be every six months. If my book fails of success, the loss falls where it ought to do. The same motives which inclined me first to offer you this trifle, incline me to give you the whole profits of the sale (except what Mr. Hinxman sells here, which will be a great many), and to have them sold only at your shop upon the usual terms in these cases.

Dodsley evidently was willing to proceed on these terms, and sometime in December the books were placed on sale in York and copies were sent down to London.

If Sterne had intended to drop a bombshell into the minor muddle of York's local scandal, he succeeded admirably. No sooner had the books made their appearance than tongues started wagging. Dr. Topham was easily recognizable in Didius, but there were several claimants, at least, for the doubtful honor of being Dr. Slop's original. Burton professed to see no likeness between himself and Sterne's paper effigy, and another doctor, taking the

insult to himself, protested to Sterne. The author assured
the physician that he had not insulted him, but the man
persisted in his belief Sterne had held him up to ridicule.

"Are you a man-midwife?" Sterne asked.

The physician answered that he was not.

"Are you a Catholic?" the author went on.

"No."

"Were you ever splashed?" Sterne asked then, referring
to an incident in the book, in which Dr. Slop figured.

The physician seized upon this incident to support his
claim. "Yes," he shouted, "and that is the very thing you
have taken advantage of to expose me!"

At this, Sterne became disgusted with the man, and
warned him, "Sir, I have not hurt you yet, but take care.
I am not born yet—heaven knows what I will do in the
next two volumes."

But York relished the volumes, as any gossip-loving com-
munity would. People spent their time deciphering the
incidents referred to and conjecturing on the true identity
of the characters. Legends, some true, many pure myths,
grew up regarding indignant citizens who waited on the
author to protest; the one quoted above is an example.
Sterne thoroughly enjoyed his new found notoriety.

The book had been on sale several weeks in York before it was offered to the public in London. Even though
Dodsley had agreed to handle the book, he was still extremely doubtful of its success in the city. Londoners
could hardly be expected to understand or be interested
in York gossip, and in the city the book would be judged
in other lights. It was an odd performance, full of typographical quirks, misplaced chapters, a dedication in the
middle of the first volume; its punctuation was odd, the
structure seemed to follow no known rules of composition
or syntax; there was almost no action, for although it

began ostensibly by relating the birth of Tristram, the two volumes ended with the child still unborn. Most of the book was taken up in conversations, in digressions in which the author expressed his opinions. In one of these he had laid down his credo as an author:

> ——Writers of my stamp have one principle in common with painters. Where an exact copying makes our pictures less striking, we choose the less evil; deeming it even more pardonable to trespass against truth, than beauty.
>
> .   .   .
>
> Writing, when properly managed (as you may be sure I think mine is) is but a different name for conversation. As no one, who knows what he is about in good company, would venture to talk all;——so no author, who understands the just boundaries of decorum and good-breeding, would presume to think all: The truest respect which you can pay to the reader's understanding, is to halve this matter amicably, and leave him something to imagine, in his turn, as well as yourself.

Sterne had risked more than is generally appreciated in these volumes. His ecclesiastical superiors had already made it clear that they viewed his attempts at satirical writing in poor taste. In *Tristram Shandy* he went beyond the bounds ordinarily vouchsafed the clergy, even in a period somewhat more lenient in that respect than our own. Several brother clerics took him to task on this score, and his friend Fothergill advised him to "get your preferment first, and then write and welcome." Certain it is that if the book had not found great favor, Sterne had irrevocably closed the door of church advancement.

So it was with mingled fear, anxiety, and pride that Sterne awaited the London debut of his brain-child. The new decade ushered Tristram into the city. On January

1, 1760, the *London Chronicle* carried a small advertisement:

This day was published,

Printed on a superfine writing paper, and a new Letter, in two Volumes, Price 5s. neatly bound,

The LIFE and OPINIONS of
TRISTRAM SHANDY, Gent.

York, printed for and sold by John Hinxman (Successor to the late Mr. Hildyard) Bookseller in Stonegate: J. Dodsley in Pallmall and M. Cooper in Paternoster-row, London: and by all the Booksellers.

Thus *Tristram Shandy* ventured into the city.

X

Tristram in London

ALTHOUGH *Tristram Shandy* made its way hesitantly into London, Sterne did not, by any means, leave the entire matter to chance. Kitty de Fourmantelle had made several influential friends in London, in the course of her performances, and among them were two men whose tastes played a large part in swaying public demand. These two were Richard Berenger, a young man-about-town, and David Garrick, the actor. To one of these men "dear Kitty" addressed a letter on the very day when the London newspapers noted the publication of *Tristram Shandy;* in view of subsequent events, it seems more probable that the letter went to Garrick, but both the actor and Berenger championed the volumes and both became Sterne's friends. The evidence seems to indicate that Kitty's letter was dictated—perhaps even written in its entirety—by Sterne (hardly a grave sin in our own day, when "publicity" is the very life-blood of literature). But if Sterne actually wrote the letter, he did an excellent imitation of a modest young lady:

> Sir,
> I dare say you will wonder to receive an Epistle from me, and the Subject of it will surprise you still more, because it is to tell you something about Books.

There are two volumes just published here, which
have made a great noise, and have had a prodigious
run; for, in two days after they came out, the Bookseller sold two hundred, and continues selling them
very fast. It is the *Life and Opinions of Tristram
Shandy*, which the Author told me last night at our
Concert he had sent up to London, so perhaps you
have seen it; If you have not seen it, pray get it and
read it, because it has a great character as a witty
smart Book, and if you think so, your good word in
Town will do the Author, I am sure, great service.
You must understand he is a kind and generous
friend of mine, whom Providence has attach'd to me
in this part of the World, where I came a stranger—
and I could not think how I could make a better return, than by endeavouring to make you a Friend to
him and his performance; this is all my excuse for
this Liberty, which I hope you will excuse. His name
is Sterne, a Gentleman of great Preferment, and a
Prebendary in the Church of York, and has a great
character, in these parts, as a man of Learning and
Wit; the Graver people, however, say 'tis not fit for
young Ladies to read his Book, so perhaps you'l think
it not fit for a young Lady to recommend it; however
the Nobility and great Folks stand up mightily for it,
and say 'tis a good Book, tho' a little tawdry in some
places.—I am, dear Sir, your most obedient and humble servant.

To Garrick, shortly afterwards, went copies of the two
volumes, as a gift of the author. Garrick read the books,
was pleased by them, and recommended them to his circle.
The actor was at the height of his fame. The audiences
which assembled in the Drury Lane Theater included the
most fashionable men and women of London. To them
Garrick's taste was equivalent to authority, and Garrick's
praise was the arbiter's law. So within a few weeks the
book began to find its way into the homes of the great.

The more daring read and discussed it in the drawing rooms; the more timid read it in their bedrooms. The moralists found it shocking; the blasé found it boring; but the majority of the fashionable, although puzzled by it, chuckled over its double-entendre and found its vulgarities delightful. The York controversies troubled them not a whit, and London accepted the performance at its face value.

The London magazines, not knowing quite what to make of the amazing volumes, praised them in conventional, high-sounding, terms—of the sort that working reviewers are prone to use when the significance of any work escapes them. But this kind of praise might have been enough to kill the book in its infancy, had it not—fortunately—been met with a brickbat for every bouquet. The moralists denounced it as vulgar, but in that day, as in this, such denunciation was a boon to the sales. A more serious charge came from a section of intellectuals; this was the charge of dullness, and its typical expression is found in a letter of Horace Walpole:

> At present nothing is talked of, nothing admired, but what I can not help calling a very insipid and tedious performance: it is a kind of novel, called *The Life and Opinions of Tristram Shandy;* the great humour of which consists in the whole narration always going backwards. I can conceive a man saying that it would be droll to write a book in that manner, but have no notion of his persevering in executing it. It makes one smile two or three times at the beginning, but in recompense makes one yawn for two hours.

The physicians in London, like those in York, were resentful of Sterne's slurs on the medical profession. Not content with his lampooning of Dr. Burton, Sterne had seized upon a notorious "foible" of a well known physician, who had recently died. In the character of Dr. Kunastrokius, Sterne attacked the late Dr. Mead, and brought down upon his head the wrath of those who felt he had acted unfairly in insulting the memory of a dead man. From a London physician came a letter of sharp protest, based upon the adage *De mortuis nil nisi bonum*— of the dead speak only good. Sterne's defense of himself against this charge was long and often heated, but it is so typical of the man in this period that some parts of it must be quoted. He analyzes with the clarity of an iconoclast the Latin truism:

> I declare I have considered the wisdom and foundation of it over and over again, as dispassionately and charitably as a good Christian can, and, after all, I can find nothing in it, or make more of it than a nonsensical lullaby of some nurse, put into Latin by some pedant to be chanted by some hypocrite to the end of the world, for the consolation of departing lechers . . . . and reason and common sense tell me, that if the characters of past ages and men are to be drawn at all, they are to be drawn like themselves; that is, with their excellencies, and with their foibles—and it is as much a piece of justice to the world, and to virtue too, to do the one as the other.—

The physician had accused the author of "cowardice and injustice," and Sterne took up the charge:

> But why cowardice? "because 'tis not courage to attack a dead man who can't defend himself."—But why do you doctors of the faculty attack such a one with your incision-knife? Oh! for the good of the living. —'Tis my plea.—But I have something more to say in my behalf—and it is this—I am not guilty of the charge—though defensible. I have not cut up Doctor Kunastrokius at all.—I have just scratched him—and that scarce skin-deep.

The physician had insulted Sterne by intimating that the author indulged in cheap sensationalism to increase the sale of the volumes. Sterne answered hotly:

> —The consolation you give me, that my book, how-ever, will be read enough "to answer my design of raising a tax upon the public"—is very unconsolatory —to say nothing how very mortifying! By H——n! an author is worse treated than a common *****
> at this rate—"*You will get a penny by your sins, and that's enough.*" Upon this chapter let me comment. —That I proposed laying the world under contribu-tion when I set pen to paper,—is what I own, and I suppose I may be allow'd to have that view in my head, in common with every other writer, to make my labor of advantage to myself.
>
> Do you not do the same? but I beg I may add, that whatever views I had of that kind, I had other views —the first of which was, the hopes of doing the world good, by ridiculing what I thought deserving of it— or of disservice to sound learning—

His correspondent has said flatly that the "book can not be put into the hands of any woman of character"! Here Sterne releases the flood of his resentment in sarcasm:

> (I hope you except widows, doctor—for they are not *all* so squeamish, but I am told they are all really of my party, in return for some good offices done their interests in the 176th page of my second volume.) But for the chaste married, and chaste unmarried part of the sex—they must not read my book! Heaven forbid the stock of chastity should be lessened by the Life and Opinions of Tristram Shandy—yes, his opin-ions—it would certainly debauch 'em! God take them under his protection in this fiery trial, and send us plenty of Duennas to watch the workings of their humors till they have safely got through the whole work. If this will not be sufficient, may we have plenty of Sangrados to pour in plenty of cold water,

till this terrible fermentation is over. . . . I fear you think me very poor, or in debt—I thank God, though I don't abound—that I have enough for a clean shirt every day—and a mutton chop—and my contentment, with this, has thus far (and I hope ever will) put me above stooping an inch for it. . . . Curse on it, I like it not to that degree, nor envy *(you may be sure)* any man who kneels in the dirt for it—so that howsoever I may fall short of the ends proposed in commencing author—I enter this *protest,* first, that my end was *honest;* and, secondly, that I wrote not to be *fed,* but to be *famous.*

Sterne's protest that he had a serious purpose and plan in mind is more than a little justified. In his letter to Dodsley, he had intimated that new volumes would be forthcoming every six months, and throughout the book the author promises new developments, new adventures. All of this seems to indicate that *Tristram Shandy,* as it finally appeared in print, was not the hodge-podge it must have seemed to many. From what had started purely as a match for the local powder-box, Sterne had conceived a broader scope. *Tristram Shandy* was to be the vehicle to carry Sterne's revolt against the hypocrisies and follies of his age. In a large measure Sterne failed, for in adopting the character of jester to the fashionable, he set himself a narrow boundary for his efforts. But within the limitations he set himself, Sterne gave to his age and to future generations much that was sound and admirable.

But in the early spring of 1760, all this was still in the future. Sterne lived those months in a terrible state of fear and anxiety, as a careful reading of the reply to his London critic reveals. Against the independence of spirit which he claimed vaguely as his goal was set the more vivid fear that he had overstepped the bounds with his writing. After all, he still wore the cloak of the Church

of England, and his superiors in the Church must sooner
or later be reckoned with. The response from London,
although better in many respects than he might well have
expected, was not too reassuring. The reviews thus far
had been favorable, and there were satisfying comparisons
of Sterne with Swift, and even Rabelais. But against this
was the undertone of disapproval of those who had been
shocked and felt their sensibilities insulted. Their protest could be expected to register heavily in the Church.

Nor had the venture, thus far, been of any benefit to the
parson financially. The hundred pounds advanced him
by his friend Mr. Lee, we may well imagine, had long
since been consumed in the costs of printing and binding,
while the two hundred copies sold in York, and the few
copies sent to London could have yielded but little in
return.

Nor could Sterne have found very much to console him
in events at home. Mrs. Sterne was on the road to recovery, but her illness was still a tax on the parson, with his
weak constitution. Her mother's illness had reacted badly
on Lydia, and the child suffered a blow to her health.
The family remained in York through the winter, not only
to give Mrs. Sterne the advantage of an able doctor's care,
but also to give Lydia the education that a York school
could bestow. If he could not leave his child a fortune,
Sterne declared, at least he could give her the advantages
of learning.

The weeks of February slipped away, with the news
from London sometimes encouraging, often bleak. Her
father's new found fame brought sorrow to Lydia: Her
schoolmates had taken to taunting her with the epithet of
Miss Shandy, and the resourceful Lydia set about to get
her revenge. The local story has it that she wrote love-
letters to the schoolgirls, signing the names of players in

the local theatrical company. Irate parents, finding the letters, punished the girls, and Lydia had her revenge. But some weeks later, when Sterne had gone away to London, this revenge had repercussions. The anger of the girl's parents sought out the players as a target, and the company was forced to leave the city. Lydia's guilt was discovered too late to help the actors.

Sterne had made no plans to go to London; his journey, in fact, came about by chance. He was walking on the streets of York one morning in early March, when he met Stephen Croft. Croft was preparing to go into London, and he offered to pay all of Sterne's expenses if the parson would accompany him. Tempting as the offer was, Sterne hesitated to leave his wife, in her condition. Nevertheless, he knew that the anxiety that had been gnawing at him these last two months might be stilled by a visit to the city; it required but little urging on Croft's part to persuade him. He returned home, packed a bag, and set out with his friend.

On the evening of March 4 Sterne and his companion rode into London, and Sterne began the last—and greatest —phase of his life.

XI

The Jester Is Born

IT HAS been repeated often that no writer, before or since Sterne's time, ever received such an ovation in London as that given the tall, lanky country parson. Before he had been twenty-four hours in the city, he had made new friends and had planted his feet firmly on the road to wealth and fame. Within three days he had met the highest members of London's fashionable circles, and had engagements two weeks ahead. Before his first week in the city was out, he was the subject of a thousand conversations, he had received a strange present of a purse of gold, and he had seen the church preferment long hoped for bestowed upon him. The lives of few men have been so changed in such a short time.

Consider the city at the time of Sterne's arrival. It was a period in which the pursuit of pleasure loomed large; the immoderate temper of the people was everywhere apparent. Morally, London was at a low ebb, and fashionable society was intent upon gratification of the senses. There was no hint yet of the reaction of the nineteenth century, and men and women alike enjoyed a large measure of freedom in their relations. Drinking to what would generally be considered an excess was not only fashionable, but quite proper, and guests very often left dinner parties in a drunken state. One of Garrick's biographers mentions—as a token of the actor's temperance—that he appeared on the stage intoxicated only once in the course of his career. The coffee houses were merry throughout the days and evenings with conversation and wine.

The most popular diversion in London was card playing, in which both men and women participated almost to the degree of a passion. The wealthy gambled for stakes that were incredibly high, and even the middle classes gambled for stakes far beyond their means. From October to May, the months of the London "season," the fashionable and wealthy quarters of the city were mad with the pursuit of pleasure. Bartholomew Fair, May Fair and Southwark Fair flourished, and one of the most popular places of amusement was Ranelagh Hall in Chelsea, which had been opened in 1742.

The manners of the period were courtly and stilted, a thin veneer for the corruption and moral *laissez-faire* that lay beneath. Attempts were made by some of the social leaders to raise the intellectual status of London society, and it is a sufficient commentary on the state of affairs that when Mrs. Montagu, Sterne's cousin-by-marriage, sought to do this, she made it a first rule that card playing was to be prohibited at her parties. (Mrs. Montagu was the leader of a social set known as the "blue stockings," a title which was acquired when one of the men in the circle attended a fashionable party given by Mrs. Vesey at Bath in blue worsted stockings, instead of the black silk that fashion decreed. One can imagine the sensation that this incident created in a society guided by Lord Chesterfield's *Letters*.)

It was an age of moral and physical degradation concealed beneath a show of splendor. Both men and women engaged in great extravagances in the matter of dress and personal appearance. Men wore waistcoats and breeches of colorful silks, and women encased themselves in great hoop skirts and incredible coiffures a foot above their heads.

Nor was the pursuit of pleasure confined to the men-about-town, the wealthy and idle. The clergy were allowed a wide measure of freedom, and London had been amused by the sight of more than one gay parson. On this score alone, Sterne's escapades might have gone quite unnoticed.

In a way it is paradoxical that along with this moral freedom the age was one of hypocrisy. Yet from another point of view it is logical that where there is little morality there will be little sincerity. The theatres—even Garrick's theatre—abounded in high-flown moral pieces, which today seem, and in fact are, hopelessly dull and shallow. Goldsmith, one of the few moral landmarks of the period, himself ridiculed them, listing the maxims they taught:

> —that it is impossible to see into the ways of futurity; that punishment always attends the villain; that love is the fond soother of the human breast; that we should not resist heaven's will, for in resisting heaven's will, heaven's will is resisted: with several other sentiments equally new, delicate, and striking.

The hypocrisy of the time is nowhere better illustrated than in the fact that audiences were quite willing to accept such stupid stuff, and copious tears were shed over these tender tragedies. After the last act, the audience dried its collective tears and betook itself to its collective intrigues.

It was in the midst of this that Sterne was deposited on the first Tuesday evening of March, 1760. How Parson Yorick, with his wild, extravagant way of talking, and his fierce independence of spirit, might have fitted into this background we can only guess, for Sterne in London proved himself a master of adaptation. So quickly that we can hardly follow the transition, he stepped out of the character of Parson Yorick, and became Yorick the king's jester. The change here was infinitely subtle; yet it is so definite that it illumines many of the dark places of Sterne's subsequent career.

London, Sterne quickly discovered, was not interested in his motives as a writer; it cared not a whit for the wrongs he hoped to right with his pen. London accepted *Tristram Shandy* because the book was amusing, because it was in part risqué and its suggestiveness fell in well with the age and the temper of the people. And now it flocked to see and hear the country parson in the hope that he would be as amusing as his book. Nor did Sterne disappoint London; he put on the jester's cap and he "shandied it" day and night, week upon week.

When Sterne landed in London, he stayed with Croft at the home of one of Croft's friends. The morning after his arrival, he went to Dodsley's shop in Pall Mall, to inquire after the sale of his book. He discovered to his astonishment that there was not a copy left in all London, so steady had the demand for the volumes been. That very morning the publisher drew up a new agreement, by the terms of which Sterne was to get six hundred and thirty pounds—two hundred and fifty pounds for the copyright of the two volumes, to be published in a new edition, and three hundred and eighty pounds for the third and fourth volumes, still unwritten. In addition, Sterne was to receive the profits from the sale of the copies already disposed of. The country parson may have been a poor business man in his farming ventures, but the bargain he struck with Dodsley proved him a shrewd enough dealer in the works of his brain; the price was almost unheard of for a first work in that day. When Sterne left Dodsley, his head was in the clouds, and he walked on air. Returning to his friend Croft, he announced excitedly that he was "the richest man in Europe."

The next day Sterne called on Garrick, and the actor immediately took the country parson under his wing. Garrick gave Sterne the freedom of his theatre, introduced him to numbers of "great" people—so that, two days after he arrived in the city, Sterne could write to Kitty de Fourmantelle, "I have the greatest honors paid me & most civilities shewn me, that were ever known from the Great; and am engaged all ready to ten Noble Men and Men of fashion to dine. Mr. Garrick pays me all & more honour than I could look for." Although he had intended to take rooms in Piccadilly or the Haymarket, he ended by renting an apartment near his publisher, just off Pall Mall. Now, settled in his own rooms, Sterne knew the sensation of his greatest triumphs.

In a few days he was able to seize only a moment to write a short note to Kitty. "From morning to night," he explained, "my Lodgings, which by the by, are the genteelest in Town, are full of the greatest Company. I dined these 2 days with 2 ladies of the Bedchamber; then with Lord Rockingham, Lord Edgecomb, Lord Winchelsea, Lord Littleton, a Bishop, etc. etc. I assure you, my Kitty, that Tristram is the fashion."

His mention of dining with a Bishop is a clue to one of the strangest events of Sterne's life, and one which cast a shadow over his London triumphs. The Bishop with whom he dined was William Warburton, who had recently become Bishop of Gloucester. Warburton, author of the *Divine Legation,* and a famous figure in London, had been linked to Sterne in a rumor that was circulating through the city: Gossip had it that Sterne intended to caricature Warburton in the next installment of his book,

as the tutor of Tristram Shandy. Inasmuch as the rumor
had become strong enough to reach the ears of the Bishop
and of his friend Garrick, it seems more than likely that
Sterne indeed had some such idea in mind, and had perhaps mentioned it to one of his intimates. But about that
we can only guess. This much we know—Garrick repeated
the rumor to Sterne, with perhaps an intimation that such
a caricature would be unwise. Sterne—and here we see
the first hint of a change in character—denied the rumor.
It came to him, he told the actor in a letter, "like a cut
across my finger with a sharp pen-knife." He went even
further than was strictly necessary to deny the rumor; he
even began to profess a strong liking for Warburton and
a desire to meet him. He wrote indignantly:

> What the devil!—is there no one learned blockhead
> throughout the many schools of misapplied science
> in the Christian world, to make a *tutor* of for my
> Tristram? . . . . Are we so run out of stock, that
> there is no one lumber-headed, muddle-headed, mor-
> tar-headed, pudding-headed *chap* among our doctors?
> Is there no one single wight of much reading and no
> learning, amongst the many children in my *mother's*
> nursery, who bids high for this charge—but I must
> disable my judgment by choosing a Warburton?
> . . . . The report might draw blood, of the author of
> *Tristram Shandy*—but could not harm such a man as
> the author of *The Divine Legation*. God bless him!
>
> · · · · ·
>
> Pray, have you no interest, lateral or collateral, to
> get me introduced to his Lordship?

Garrick, happy to be the one to effect a pleasant end to
the rumor, sent Sterne's letter to the Bishop, who declared
he would be happy to meet the author of *Tristram Shandy*
—of which work he announced himself an ardent sup-

porter. Sterne went to dine with the Bishop, and in the
course of this first meeting, Warburton presented Sterne
with a purse of gold. Sterne, in his letter to Kitty, refers
very casually to this event. "I had a purse of Guineas
given me yesterday by a Bishop; all will do well in time."
But when London heard of the incident, its comment was
far from casual. The Bishop, so gossip had it, had bribed
Sterne, to dissuade him from his intention of caricaturing
Warburton. And, to do the scandalmongers full justice,
the circumstances weighed largely in their favor. The one
factor in Sterne's honor was his frankness about the affair;
if he had accepted the purse as a bribe, it seems unlikely
he would have been so open about it. However, on the
other side we have the rumor which led up to the meeting of the two men, which lends support to the bribe
gossip. Neither Sterne nor Warburton ever offered an explanation of the affair, and thus it stands today, one of the
minor mysteries of Sterne's career.

The London sequel to his affair with Kitty de Fourmantelle illustrates with great clarity the change that his London triumphs brought upon the Yorkshire parson. From
the very beginning, his letters to her from London begged
her to come to the city, to be with him in the splendor
of his victory. She made him very happy, he assured her,
by denying herself to a rival in his absence—"whilst I am
so miserable to be separated from my dear, dear Kitty, it
would have stabb'd my soul to have thought such a fellow
could have the Liberty of comeing near you." In response
to his entreaties, she wrote to say that she might come to
London, and he answered that he longed "most impatiently
to see my dear Kitty. Tell me, tell me what day or Week
this will be." In his next letter he complained, "I have
scarce time to tell you how much I love you, my dear

Kitty, & how much I pray to God that you may so live,
and so love me, as one day to share in my great good fortune."

At last his importunities brought results. Dear, dear
Kitty arrived in London, with the full expectation, no
doubt, of sharing Sterne's triumphs. But the man she met
in the city was not the unwary but admirable Parson
Yorick: this man was Jester Yorick, the literary darling of
London, companion to the great, and fool-at-large to the
nobility. The poor music hall singer, who had been his
delight in York, seemed unimportant to him here, where
great ladies toasted him every evening. The finale of this
brief drama, probably humiliating to Catherine, whose
letter had helped to open the path to this glory, is told in
a series of short notes written by Sterne. These letters are
undated, but were written no doubt about the end of
April.

My dear Kitty,
As I cannot propose the pleasure of your Company
longer than till four o'Clock this afternoon, I have
sent you a Ticket for the Play, & hope you will go
there, that I may have the satisfaction of hopeing you
are entertained when I am not. You are a most en-
gageing Creature, and I never spend an Evening with
you, but I leave a fresh part of my heart behind me.
You will get me all, piece by piece, I find, before all
is over; & yet I cannot think, how I can ever be more
than what I am at present.
P.S.—I will be with you soon after two o'Clock, if
not at two; so get your dinner over by then.

My dear Kitty,
I was so intent upon drinking my Tea with you this
Afternoon, that I forgot I had been engaged all this
Week to visit a Gentleman's Family on this day. I
think I mentioned it in the beginning of the Week,

but your dear Company put that with many other
things out of my head: I will, however, contrive to
give my dear friend a Call at 4 o'clock; tho', by the
by, I think it not quite prudent: but what has pru-
dence, my dear Girl, to do with Love? In this I have
no government, at least not half so much as I ought.

I hope my Kitty has had a good night. May all
your days and nights be happy! Some time it may
& will be more in my power to make them so.

Adieu!

If I am prevented calling at 4, I will call at 7.

However, it appeared that Jester Sterne had more government in the matter than he would have been willing to
admit. The final note in this revealing trilogy offers eloquent proof:

My dear Kitty,
If it would have saved my life, I have not had one
hour or half hour in my power since I saw you on
Sunday; else my dear Kitty may be sure I should not
have been thus absent. Every minute of this day &
tomorrow is pre-engaged, that I am as much a pris-
oner as if I was in Jayl. I beg, dear Girl, you will
believe I do not spend an hour where I wish, for I
wish to be with you always: but fate orders my steps,
God knows how for the present.

Adieu! Adieu!

On Friday, at 2 o'clock, I will see you.

Perhaps Sterne saw his "dear Kitty" at two o'clock on
Friday; perhaps not. We can not tell, for here the story,
as far as Sterne is concerned, ended. Kitty de Fourmantelle never again entered his life physically, although in
later installments of *Tristram Shandy* the memory of her
swept over him in brief, bitter moments. He may have
met her several times in his various visits to London, and
he may have written a lyric for her to sing, but that love
so great it was little short of "distraction," was over. Her

place may have been occupied in the few weeks that remained of the London interlude by one of the "great" women, at whose altar Sterne had made himself a devotee.

How strong was the attachment between Sterne and his "dear, dear Kitty"? Sterne's academic biographers have wrangled long over the question of whether his extra-domestic loves were "innocent indiscretions"—*i.e.*, "platonic" —or serious affairs—*i.e.*, sexual affairs—as though they were judges sitting to hear a charge of adultery. Unfortunately for this attitude, we shall never know what the truth is. If we accept a statement made by Sterne in his *Journal to Eliza*, he possessed no woman sexually, not even his wife, in the last fifteen years of his life. On the other hand, there is the evidence of a letter written in Latin to John Hall-Stevenson in 1761, in which Sterne confesses that his wife no longer attracts him sexually and the "devil of love" is driving him to London. However, except out of pure curiosity, the question is of little importance. From an intelligent point of view, the mere fact of a man's going to bed with a woman hardly constitutes a touchstone of love or depth of attachment. If it did, the most noble lovers would be the prostitutes and the country bumpkins who ride into town once a week to buy their sex, like groceries, across the counter.

In the face of the Latin letter to Hall and the state of morals in London at the time, it is difficult to believe that Sterne's affairs never went beyond the *tête-à-tête* stage. Fortunately, however, the question is not essential to an understanding of Sterne. It is mentioned here only because some of Sterne's commentators have concluded that his writings expressed a hidden craving for sex, never satisfied in his affairs with women. His obscenity and his sentimentality alike are tracked to their lair as sublimations of this craving. This seems, however, to be a pecu-

liarly unsatisfactory short-cut through the maze of clues
and counter-clues to Sterne's character. He must have
had plenty of opportunities in London to gratify his sexual
desires, and we can not assume with any certainty that he
did not take advantage of these opportunities. The Latin
letter to Hall is not so much the incriminating document
that Thackeray and others have made it seem, but it is a
self-revealing document. It is high time we cease viewing
Sterne through the virtuous haze of the Victorian age and
begin to see him in the light of his period—and our own.

At least one attempt has been made to explain Sterne's
life and his writing in terms of modern psychoanalysis.
The nature and peculiar composition of *Tristram Shandy,*
coupled with Sterne's obvious failure in marriage, the
Latin letter to Hall-Stevenson and the entry in the *Journal
to Eliza* provide such a convenient base for this explanation, that the temptation is great. It would be so easy to
apply a Freudian smear and turn up a culture abounding
in sex-sublimations, phallic symbols and all the other
easily-handled bric-à-brac in the shops of the psychoan-
alysts. Surely such an approach would be not without justification. But at best it would represent a half-truth.

The fact is that in many instances Sterne's obscenity was
deliberate, introduced with an eye to the popularity of his
work. Several times he made pointed references to the
necessity of pandering to the public taste; but even more
conclusive evidence is to be found in the volumes themselves. Taking each installment as a whole, the most ob-
scene is probably the second installment, comprising the
third and fourth volumes. These volumes were written
just after his return to Yorkshire, when his first London
triumph was still fresh in his mind. London had accepted
and praised the first installment of his book largely for its
suggestiveness, and he set out deliberately to accentuate

this phase in his second installment. In this installment, then, are to be found Ernulphus' oath of excommunication, with its vulgarity of language; Slawkenbergius' tale, with its double-entendre. And further evidence is to be found in the fact that the best sections of the book, almost free of suggestiveness, were written with a sojourn in France between him and his London acclaim. He wrote his final work, the *Sentimental Journey*, he admitted in the last year of his life, in part as a vindication for the indecencies of *Tristram Shandy*. So, while these indecencies are in most instances forgivable and in some cases add to the book, still Sterne recognized them as such and deliberately included them. They are not the outpourings of a sex-degenerate mind, but the calculated work of a man who began writing to be *famous*, and continued to be *fed*.

Meanwhile many new glories had been heaped upon Sterne in London. Early in March the living of Coxwould had been vacated by the death of the incumbent Vicar. The living was in the gift of Lord Fauconberg, who had been friendly to Sterne for many years. This was the very preferment which Sterne had hoped for a decade earlier; but Jaques and Archbishop Hutton had opposed him in his wish, and it had gone to another man. Now, however, all the circumstances were altered: Jaques was dead and a new Archbishop sat in Bishopthorpe. Sterne was no longer an obscure clergyman, but a great literary figure and the toast of London. Fauconberg did not hesitate over the matter. As soon as news of the incumbent's death reached him in London, he named Sterne for the place, and Archbishop Gilbert approved the appointment. Sterne was overjoyed by this stroke of fortune, for the living yielded one hundred and sixty pounds a year, more than the combined total of all the other ecclesiastical offices he held.

Dodsley had pushed with all speed the preparations for a new edition of *Shandy,* and Sterne secured for it what a few weeks ago he would not have dared to hope for—an illustration by Hogarth to use as a frontispiece. Sterne met the artist through Richard Berenger, and the letter from the parson to Berenger on this occasion is as Shandean a piece as ever Sterne scribbled:

My dear Berenger,

You bid me tell You all my Wants—What the Devil in Hell can the fellow want now?—By the Father of the Sciences (you know his Name) I would give both my Ears (if I was not to lose my Credit by it) for no more than ten Strokes of *Howgarth's* witty Chissel, to clap at the Front of my next Edition of *Shandy.*— The Vanity of a pretty Girl in the Hey day of her Roses & Lillies, is a fool to that of Author of my Stamp—Oft did Swift sigh to Pope in these words— Orna me—Unite something of yours to mine, to trans- mit us down together hand in hand to futurity. The loosest sketch in Nature, of Trim's reading the ser- mon to my Father &c; would do the Business—& it would mutually illustrate his System & mine—But my dear Shandy with what face——I would hold out my lank Purse—I would Shut my Eyes—, & You should put in your hand, & take out what you liked for it— Ignoramus! Fool! Blockhead! Symoniack!—This Grace is not to be *bought* with money—perish thee & thy Gold with thee!

What Shall we do? I have the worst face in the world to ask a favour with—& besides I would not propose a disagreeable thing to one I so much admire for the whole world—but you can say anything—You are an impudent honest Dog & can'st set a face upon a bad Matter—prithee sally out to Leicester fields, and when You have knockd at the door (for you must

knock first) and art got in—begin thus "—Mr. Hogarth, I have been with my friend Shandy this morning"—but go on your own Way—as I shall do mine
I esteem you & am my dear Mentor

                                Yours most Shandaically
                                L Sterne

The "impudent honest Dog"—that Dick Berenger, who
is remembered by the diarists of the period as polished,
elegant, and chivalrous—carried Sterne's message to the famous illustrator, and Hogarth responded generously. He
sent back, without charge, an illustration of the very scene
chosen by Sterne—the scene of Trim reading the sermon
on *The Abuses of Conscience*. Sterne wrote a dedication
for the edition to Pitt, who was yet to become Prime Minister. With these additions, the second edition appeared
the first week in April. So great was the demand for the
volumes that the second edition was exhausted shortly,
and two more editions were required before the year was
out.

With the new printing off his hands, Sterne set to work
immediately on a new project. Dodsley had agreed to
bring out some of Sterne's sermons in book form, and
Sterne began the process of selecting and editing them.
A new contract with Dodsley brought Sterne two hundred
pounds more than had originally been agreed upon, and
the author's prospects appeared brighter daily. *The Sermons of Mr. Yorick,* fifteen in all, came off the press late
in May and were offered for sale in two volumes, with a
portrait of Sterne, painted by Reynolds and engraved by
Ravenet, as a frontispiece. The books had been sub-
scribed for by more than six hundred persons, including
the greatest names of the realm. A glance through the
table of contents reveals what a variety of subjects Sterne
chose to present. In the first volume we find *Inquiry after*

Happiness, The House of Feasting and the House of Mourning Described, Philanthropy Recommended, Self-Knowledge, The Case of Elijah and the Widow of Zarephath Considered, Pharisee and Publican in the Temple, and *Vindication of Human Nature.* The titles in the second volume were *Time and Chance, The Character of Herod, Job's Account of the Shortness and Troubles of Life Considered, Evil-Speaking, Joseph's History Considered, Duty of Setting Bounds to Our Desires, Self-Examination,* and *Job's Expostulation with His Wife.* They were the cream of Yorick's ecclesiastical crop, and he was proud of the volumes.

However, despite the noble patronage under which the volumes were published and the excellence of the sermons, Sterne was under some apprehension about the title. His adoption of the name Yorick was well enough for the author of a risqué novel, but he was afraid that it might be looked upon as a profaning of the sermons. To guard against this, he inserted an additional title page: "Sermons by Laurence Sterne, A. M. Prebendary of York, and Vicar of Sutton on the Forest, and of Stillington near York." He explained his action in a preface, which said in part:

> The sermon which gave rise to the publication of these, having been offer'd to the world as a sermon of *Yorick's,* I hope the most serious reader will find nothing to offend him, in my continuing these two volumes under the same title: lest it should be otherwise, I have added a second title page with the real name of the author:—

With the publication of the volumes, he found that his fears were indeed justified. The reviewers, while praising the sermons, in some instances took him to task for having besmirched his robes with a jester's name. But on the whole the sermons were very well received, and many who had professed themselves aghast at the liberties of *Tristram Shandy* were inclined to forgive the author. And it can be said for the books that they are still highly readable today, and well worth the reading.

Before we close the drama of Sterne's London triumph, there is one scene of pomp and pageantry that engages our attention. Sterne had been greatly flattered by the notice accorded him by the young Duke of York, brother of the future King George III. The young man, who had something of a reputation for wildness and pleasure-seeking, invited Sterne to dine with him, and together they attended several social functions. Thus Sterne made his way into court circles, and in the first week in May, before his sermons had been published, the author was invited to Windsor, to witness the ceremonies marking the installation of three men as Knights of the Garter. One of the men to be so honored was Lord Rockingham, who has already been mentioned in these pages as one of the noblemen who had invited Sterne to dine. It was in Rockingham's party that Sterne traveled to Windsor. The procession, the installation, and the brilliant social affairs attending the ceremony lasted nearly a week, and the pageantry was as colorful as it could only be in a land that loved the traditional pomp of royalty. Sterne was dazzled by it all, especially by the many famous statesmen, including Pitt, whom he met there.

Returning to London, Sterne found many things awaiting his attention, and little time for them. There were, as usual, a dozen dinner engagements to be met, a special sermon to preach before the judges, his volumes of sermons to be brought out. But, by the time the sermons appeared, in the latter part of May, he was free of his engagements and ready for the journey home. With a part of the money this trip had netted him he bought a carriage and a pair of fine horses, as befitted a gentleman who had been the rage of a London season. Much of his money had gone on clothing, and he was preparing to return to York well turned out.

On Monday of the last week in May, Sterne ended his three months in the city. Outfitted in his new clothes, carrying with him some of his new books for his York friends, he climbed into his smart new carriage. The two prancing horses turned northward, and the curtain came down on the most amazing literary comedy of all time.

THE JESTER IS BORN

XII

"The Sweet Retirement"

As STERNE drove leisurely northward to rejoin his family, he had much to think about. In retrospect there were several things to mar the perfection of his London visit. The ghost of Warburton's purse of guineas had by no means been laid, and occasionally a wave of remorse may have come over him for the manner in which he had received Kitty de Fourmantelle. But there were blots more concrete than these upon the London vista—and more public. Sterne was troubled by the reception his book had had at the hands of the littérateurs. While the public flocked to buy it, the literary leaders took little notice of it, except occasionally to damn it faintly. Johnson and Goldsmith were outspoken in their disfavor of the book and its author, and to the end Johnson maintained this dislike, Goldsmith, in later articles, attacked the book for the breaks and digressions of its style, as well as for the indecencies of its jests. During the London season and for months afterwards, Sterne was pestered by a flood of pamphlets attacking *Tristram Shandy* or profiting from its popularity by imitating its style and manner. So pestiferous did these parasites become, in fact, that Dodsley was forced to resort to advertising to protect Sterne and the publishing firm against these spurious booklets. The weekly and monthly critics too became bolder as the book gained wider attention. Although they had at first been able to make little of *Tristram Shandy,* and were rather inclined to pass it off with the traditional banalities of the working press, they became more venturesome as they saw its popularity grow. Some found his humor antedated, others attacked the typographical affectations. Sterne felt the sting of their rebukes and the coldness of his reception at the hands of other writers, and in his next installment of *Shandy* he brought the force of his ridicule to bear upon his critics:

—their heads, Sir, are stuck so full of rules and compasses, and have that eternal propensity to apply them upon all occasions, that a work of genius had better go to the devil at once, than stand to be pricked and tortured to death by 'em.

And what of this new book the whole world makes such a rout about?——Oh! 'tis out of all plumb, my Lord,——quite an irregular thing!——not one of the angles at the four corners was a right angle.——I had my rule and compasses, etc., my Lord, in my pocket. ——Excellent critic!

—And for the epic poem your lordship bid me look at—upon taking the length, breadth, height, and depth of it, and trying them at home upon an exact scale of Bossu's——'tis out, my Lord, in every one of its dimensions.—Admirable connoisseur!

But worse than any of these, Sterne's reputation had been injured by an article appearing in the *Royal Female Magazine,* written by a Dr. John Hill, whose fame was bound up with a medical nostrum of doubtful standing. This article was widely copied in the newspapers of London, and it stands as probably the first "human interest" story on the life and habits of a literary celebrity. (Thus we track the current effusions of publicity men to their lair!) To the delight of many hundreds of readers, Dr. Hill's article abounded in anecdotes of the man who held the attention of all London, but unfortunately for Sterne the information was grossly inaccurate. The article repeated the story of Warburton's purse of guineas and several other tales damaging to Sterne's character. Some people actually accused Sterne of having written the article himself, to gain further notoriety. This Sterne denied hotly, in a letter to his friend Croft. "The people of York," he wrote, "are very uncharitable to suppose any man so gross a beast as to pen such a character of himself.— In this great town, no soul ever suspected it, for a thousand reasons;—could they suppose I should be such a fool as to fall foul upon Dr. Warburton, my best friend, by representing him so weak a man,—or by telling such a lie of him,—as his giving me a purse, to buy off his tutorship for Tristram!—or should I be fool enough to own I had taken his purse for that purpose!"

Physically the London visit had also been harmful to Sterne. His health, never excellent, had been undermined by the continual round of activities in the city—late hours, exposure to London's late winter weather, and excessive drinking had left their mark upon him. He was glad, for his health's sake, to be leaving the city, and he looked forward to his new retreat in the Coxwould parsonage.

But the greatest change in Sterne was in his attitude of mind. He had fallen readily into the character of the town's jester, and he was about to take up his pen in that character. He was none the less a satirist now than he had been when he started to work on *Shandy*, but he knew better how to please the public that paid for his work. He knew that the coarse and suggestive parts of the first installment had insured its success—damn it as they might in the drawing rooms, they would chuckle over it in their bedrooms—he knew it and said as much. So he was prepared to sacrifice subtlety for coarseness. Sterne was gratified but not duped by his London success; he knew only too well—now that he had time to reflect—the character of his reception in the city. He often compared himself to a fashionable courtesan who enjoys great favor while she is in style—but let a few weeks pass and the fickle admirers would forget her. He hoped to make the public pay for its courting of him while the mood was upon them, and he realized vaguely that if his book was destined to survive him, it would not be because the town had heaped favors upon its author. But his thoughts of immortality came later; now he was concerned with pleasing the fickle friends his book had brought him.

Arrived in York, he found his wife recovered completely from her illness and her delusions, and he was amused by the story of Lydia's love-letter revenge on her school-mates. He spent several weeks in York, clearing up business matters and arranging to remove his family from Sutton to Coxwould. From York he sent the two volumes of sermons to his benefactor Warburton. By the beginning of the summer season he had made the necessary arrangements and had taken over the curacy of Coxwould. Although he might ordinarily have been able to take active charge of all three of his parishes, he wanted to occupy himself with his writing, and he secured a curate for Sutton and Stillington. This left only Coxwould in his direct charge, and he estimated that, even with the expense of the curate, he would be richer by seventy pounds a year for the new curacy.

"A sweet retirement," Sterne called his new home. It was "Shandy Castle" to him, and later "Shandy Hall," a title it continued to hold through the years. Coxwould, about fifteen miles from York, was situated high up among green hills, a relief to Sterne after the years spent in Sutton's swampy valleys, and a tonic to his failing health. The parsonage was a long, low structure, with sharp-angled tiled roofs. Three gables and as many chimneys added to its picturesqueness; at one end a heavy, broad stone buttress pyramided upward from the ground, to end as a kitchen chimney. A pathway led to an iron gate set in its stone and iron fence, and the whole, against a background of old trees and verdant shrubbery presented a pretty picture of rural comfort. Within were wainscotted walls and low ceilings. One room was set apart as Sterne's study; here were his books—seven hundred, which he purchased "dog-cheap" at an auction. Here was the desk at which he wrote seven volumes of *Tristram Shandy* and the beginning of the *Sentimental Journey*, which might have overshadowed *Tristram* had he lived to complete it. Here was the double-knobbed chair in which he sat to compose, and the fireplace at which he stirred up new wild jests for his pen.

He began at once on the new installment of *Shandy*. The picture comes clearly of the lank parson, with a wild gleam of deviltry in his eye, dipping his pen in the inkwell, spilling half of it carelessly over his paper, his desk, and his clothing; we see him bending close over his paper, writing rapidly, breaking his lines of manuscript with dashes and asterisks. Lydia comes in sometimes to help copy the scribbled pages, and often in the evenings Mrs. Sterne sits beside the fire and knits, while her husband reads her the chapters he has added to the rapidly growing pile of manuscript.

Within a mile lies Lord Fauconberg's estate, and the nobleman often invited the parson to dine and spend an evening in pleasant conversation. Sterne's company was as acceptable to them here as in the city: more so, for he shone to greatest advantage in a small, intimate group. Despite his reputation, he was often awkward and ill at ease in a large company. But here at Coxwould he was among friends of many years' standing, and their evenings together were thoroughly enjoyable.

The parson was generous with his new-found wealth. For Mrs. Sterne he bought a carriage, so she could enjoy the drive to Lord Fauconberg's estate. Lydia rode out on her new pony. Even the parishioners enjoyed Sterne's bounty, and the meanest of them had a deep admiration for the new parson. At Sutton, Sterne found dislike among his "flock"; at Coxwould he was on the best of terms with them. On the occasion of the coronation of the new king, George III, Sterne roasted a whole ox, at his own expense, for a great public celebration in the village square. His people showed their appreciation. "Not a parishioner catches a hare, or a rabbit, or a trout," he wrote, "but he brings it as an offering to me."

Pretty pictures, these, but there were dissonances to mar the harmony of that first Coxwould summer. No sooner had Sterne settled down to the second installment of *Shandy*, than he received a letter from his patron Warburton, in acknowledgement of the volumes of sermons Sterne had sent him. The Bishop now showed that he had no real understanding of Sterne, nor any real friendship for him. He consoled Sterne for the rebukes of the critics, and warned him of the inconstancy of the public. Then he launched a moral broadside at the author:

> You have it in your power to make that which is an amusement to yourself and others useful to both; at least you should, above all things, beware of its becoming hurtful to either by any violations of decency and good manners; but I have already taken such re-

peated liberties of advising you on that head, that to
say more were needless, or perhaps unacceptable.

That he mistook Sterne's talent is evident enough, for it
was no part of Sterne's purpose or desire to write innocuous pieces for the moral edification of his readers. But,
unfortunately for Warburton's cause, he erred in the tone
of his letter, for if anything could be calculated to incite
resentment in Sterne, it was this air of moral advice and
consolation. His answer to the Bishop was defiant and
resentful in tone; he restrained himself, to address Warburton with the respect due a Bishop, but there is, none-
theless, an unmistakable note of distrust and defiance. He
said he would not willingly offend by a violation of decency, but he pointed out that he could not well "mutilate
everything" in *Tristram* "down to the prudish humor of
every particular." The bitterness of the old Yorick is in
his promise: "I will, however, do my best, though laugh,
my lord, I will, and as loud as I can, too."

Warburton replied to this, telling Sterne to laugh, "in
good time" but always "in good company where priests
and virgins may be present." He warned the author subtly
to consider his chances for church preferment and reminded him "that a man was never writ out of the reputation he had fairly won but by himself."

The entire correspondence seems, at first sight, to be so
admirable on Warburton's part, demonstrating such excellent reserve and a spirit of friendliness, that it lends
color to a charge of ingratitude against Sterne: that he
should have received with such ill grace the efforts of a
friend to aid him. But Sterne interpreted the correspondence otherwise—as an effort of the Bishop to save his own
face. For Warburton had appeared publicly as Sterne's
patron, and if the author disgraced himself it would reflect
back upon his sponsor. That Sterne's interpretation and

defiant response were justified is shown by a letter from
Warburton to Garrick about their mutual friend: "I heard
enough of his conduct in town," the Bishop wrote, "since
I left it to make me think he would soon lose the fruits
of all the advantage he had gained by a successful effort,
*and would disable me from appearing as his friend and
well-wisher."* (The italics are mine.) To pursue the thing
further, when Sterne persisted in disagreeing with Warburton, the Bishop withdrew his patronage and denounced
the author as "an irrecoverable scoundrel." Sterne remembered his turncoat patron with a line in the fourth
volume of *Shandy:* "But your horse throws dirt," he ad-
monished Tristram, "——see, you have splashed a bishop."

Meanwhile, Sterne was working away at furious speed,
"curveting and frisking it away, two up and two down,
without looking once behind, or even on one side of me."
By August 3, he had completed the third volume, and was
writing to his "witty widow," Mrs. Fergusson, with whom
he corresponded over a period of many years, that his
"brains are as dry as a squeez'd orange." But there was
another volume to be written before the winter season,
and Sterne set off again at a fast pace. By October 9,
Dodsley was already making plans for the new installment,
and had inserted an advertisement in the *London Chronicle:*

> The public is desired to take notice, that the third
> and fourth volumes of "Tristram Shandy" by the au-
> thor of the first and second volumes, will be pub-
> lished about Christmas next. Printed for R. & J.
> Dodsley, in Pall Mall—

Some time in November the two new volumes were ready
for the press, and Sterne made his plans to return to London. His health continued poor, and a season in London
could not prove other than harmful, but nothing would

deter him, and he looked forward with keen anticipation to another triumph in the city. Leaving his parish business in the hands of his curates, he left Yorkshire for London in the latter part of December, and by Christmas Day his letter to Stephen Croft reveals him again embroiled in an endless round of activities, always in a "continual hurry since the moment I arrived here—what with my books, and what with visitors and visitings—"

He found an unusual interest in the political atmosphere. For the first time in many years there sat on the English throne a king who could speak English, who was born and reared in England. The first two Georges had been German in attitude as well as origin; they had ruled only by sufferance of Parliament, and the throne had been stripped of every pretense of power. Parliament, by processes of corruption and bribery, had become a mere mockery of representative government. Into this scene came George III, determined to reassert the prerogatives of the throne and re-establish the powers of the monarch. Sterne's letter to Croft is a reflection of a section of the liberal view of the new king:

> The King seems resolved to bring all things back to their original principles, and to stop the torrent of corruption and laziness. He rises every morning at six to do business—rides out at eight to the minute—returns at nine to give himself up to the people. By persisting, 'tis thought he will oblige his Ministers and dependents to dispatch affairs with him many hours sooner than of late—and 'tis much to be questioned whether they will not be enabled to wait upon him sooner, by being freed from long levees of their own, and applications; which will in all likelihood be transferred from them directly to himself—the present system being to remove that phalanx of great people, which stood betwixt the throne and the subjects, and suffer them to

have immediate access, without the intervention of a cabal—(this is the language of others): however, the King gives everything himself, knows every thing, and weighs everything maturely, and then is inflexible— this puts old stagers off their game—how it will end we are all in the dark.

Sterne, who had gained the favor of the new king's brother the preceding spring, seems to have mingled in court circles, and went to the House of Commons to hear his admired Pitt debate in defense of the Prussian war, which England had supported. But Sterne was disappointed when Pitt failed to appear upon the floor—"a political fit of the gout seized the great combatant," he told Croft. The rumor filtered up to York that Sterne had made himself unwelcome at court, and he found something humorous in the idea that he should be the subject of such a rumor—it exaggerated his importance, he assured Croft:

> You made me and my friends here very merry with the accounts current at York, of my being forbid the Court—but they do not consider what a considerable person they make of me, when they suppose either my going, or my not going there, is a point that ever enters the King's head—and for those about him, I have the honor either to stand so personally well known to them, or to be so well represented by those of the first rank, as to fear no accident of that kind.

The work of seeing *Shandy* through the process of printing went on through the month of January. Sterne expected the book to be on sale by the twentieth of the month, but it was a week later before it made its appearance. He had expected and prepared himself for the attacks of the critics, but even he could not have foreseen the rage of professional abuse that now greeted him. "I shall be attacked and pelted, either from cellars or garrets, write what I will," he had written Croft before the new installment appeared, "—and besides, must expect to have a party against me of many hundreds—who either do not —or will not laugh. 'Tis enough if I divide the world;—at least I will rest contented with it."

The appearance of the new installment divided the world of readers—but there was no such division among the professional critics and writers. They were unanimous in their dissent, and Sterne found himself the subject of vituperation and odious comparison. The occasional voice raised in his defense sounded weak and helpless in the tumult. But the critics raged impotently; they could not stem the public demand for *Tristram*, and Sterne was able to write in triumph a few short weeks after the third and fourth volumes were published, that "One half of the town abuse my book as bitterly, as the other half cry it up to the skies—the best is, they abuse and buy it, and at such a rate, that we are going on with a second edition, as fast as possible."

Nevertheless, he was stung by the sharpness of the attack, and although he never exposed his wounds publicly, yet we can read much between the lines. There is resentment at what he felt to be an injustice in his protest to his York friend: "If my enemies knew, that by this rage of abuse and ill-will, they were effectually serving the interests both of myself and my works, they would be more quiet—but it has been the fate of my betters, who have found, that the way to fame, is like the way to heaven— through much tribulation—and till I shall have the honour to be as much maltreated as Rabelais and Swift were, I must continue humble;—for I have not filled up the measure of half their *persecutions*."

In most respects, however, the second London season was a re-enactment of the first. He found himself again "fourteen dinners deep engaged," and many new friends had arisen to honor him in the city. This time he did not limit himself to three months, but stretched his London visit out to nearly six months. The first edition of the new *Shandy* was exhausted in the early spring, and in May a second edition made its appearance. Sterne's progress was accompanied, as it was the year before, by a number of pamphlets in imitation of his book, some very elaborate ones. There is no doubt that, despite the critics, Sterne was still very much the style.

During the winter he was invited to preach a charity sermon for the benefit of the Foundling Hospital. Sterne, his mind full of more worldly matters, made several promises to appear, and even set a definite date—April 5. But it was early in May before he actually preached the sermon. London's fashionable leaders, who had entertained Sterne the jester at their tables came to hear Sterne the preacher plead for alms. Nor were they disappointed in the sermon, which was typical of his manner of framing sermons on paradoxes. He chose the text, *"If they hear not Moses and the prophets, neither will they be persuaded, though one should rise from the dead,"* and, interpreting the text literally, he gave his audience an account of a hypothetical instance, in which God might raise a man from the dead to serve as His messenger on earth. All in all it was a typical, sometimes amusing, performance, not among Sterne's best. But it was sufficient for the purpose, for the gratified officials of the hospital reported a collection of more than fifty-five pounds.

This was Sterne's last public appearance in London that season of which we have any record. He spent several weeks more in the city, continuing on his round of dinners and parties, so that it was well into June before he closed his accounts there, packed his portmanteau, and climbed into the carriage for Yorkshire.

not limit himself to three months, but stretched his London visit out to nearly six weeks. The first edition of

XIII

"This Cuckoldy Retreat"

STERNE looked forward to another summer in his
idyllic Coxwould "retirement." He hastened home from
London, stopping only as long as was necessary in York.
But the picture we get of him during the summer and fall
of 1761 is hardly a happy one. There are simple tableaux
occasionally showing a happy domestic scene—"My Lydia
helps to copy for me;—and my wife knits and listens as I
read her chapters"—or the merry scene in the square as the
parishioners feasted on Sterne's roast ox and blessed the
new king for the occasion. But the strain that runs
through the parson's themes of this period was one of
melancholy restlessness. In ill health, worn out by the
strenuous round of his activities in the city, he had eagerly
sought the quiet and beauty of Coxwould. Once arrived
there, he found it hard to settle down to his work again.
His illness, and the sudden change in pace, made him restless and sad; he longed for the gaiety of London, gayer
than ever that autumn with the king's coronation. Hall-
Stevenson went to London, and Sterne tormented himself
with thoughts of his friend's days and nights of happiness
in the city. His wife, although she formed a docile audience as Sterne re-read aloud the chapters for the new installment of *Tristram Shandy,* had no real interest in his
writing, and the passage of each day showed more clearly

the contrast in their interests and temperaments. Sterne's letters to Hall-Stevenson that summer and autumn are full of the strain of his discontent. Coxwould, which had seemed a kingdom of enchantment, became dull and almost unbearable; his home became a "cuckoldy retreat," and Sterne poured out his complaints in rambling letters to his brother Demoniac:

I rejoice you are in London—rest you there in peace; here 'tis the devil. You was a good prophet. I wish myself back again, as you told me I should—but not because a thin, death doing, pestiferous, north-east wind blows in a line directly from Crazy-castle turret full upon me in this cuckoldy retreat (for I value the north-east wind and all its powers not a straw)—but the transition from rapid motion to absolute rest was too violent. I should have walked about the streets of York ten days, as a proper medium to have passed through, before I entered upon my rest. I staid but a moment, and I have been here but a few, to satisfy me I have not managed my miseries like a wise man—

As he wrote, the vision of his friend going gaily upon his London rounds pierced Sterne's melancholy, and his pen cried out, "Oh, Lord! now you are going to Ranelagh tonight, and I am sitting, sorrowful as the prophet was, when the voice cried out to him and said, 'What dost thou here, Elijah?' 'Tis well the spirit does not make the same at Coxwould—for unless for the few sheep left me to take care of, in this wilderness, I might as well, nay better, be at Mecca."

Since her illness, Mrs. Sterne had become greatly changed. Now she was no longer shrill and quarrelsome; instead she had become quiet and almost amiable. But it was the amiability of indifference she displayed. Sterne's writing hardly interested her, and we can imagine her properly shocked by the more indelicate passages in his books. In justice to her, she had little reason to interest herself in his career: his triumphs touched her only in a vague, impersonal manner. Sterne's London successes, his high friends, were only words to her; she never shared her husband's fame, or tasted the glory of his triumphs. She knew as little of the London side of her husband's life as London knew of her. Sterne's existence at this time was really a dual existence; the man who flitted gaily through London's greatest houses presented a far different exterior from the country parson who sat in his slippers before the fire in his parsonage study. If Sterne allowed his wife to see only one side of his life, she can not greatly be blamed for manifesting little interest in the other. Sterne found this indifference a great relief, for his wife now made no demands upon him, nor was he called to account for his actions. Nevertheless, he found his home dull and his wife uninspiring, in comparison with the gay ladies of the city who had showered their attentions upon him.

All that summer his eyes turned toward London. It was, as usual, a woman who accentuated the dullness of Coxwould, and made London seem a very heaven in comparison. His letters to Hall-Stevenson give us the clue. In one we find this pointed lament:

> Curse of poverty, and absence from those we love!— they are two great evils which embitter all things —and yet with the first I am not haunted much. As to matrimony, I should be a beast to rail at it, for my wife is easy—but the world is not—and had I staid from her a second longer, it would have been a burning shame—else she declares herself happier without me—but not in anger is this declaration made—but in pure sober good sense, built on sound experience—

And later—in the autumn of that year, very likely—although it has often been attributed to a later date—Sterne

penned the famous Latin letter to his "cousin Anthony."
Sterne's detractors, intent upon finding damning evidence
against him, have danced gleefully around this letter for
one hundred and fifty years. Through Victorian eyes, it
appeared a cursed, almost criminal document, for it admitted frankly that he was "more sick and tired of my
wife than ever before." Our present, more sober judgment, tells us that the letter is proof of nothing more
damaging than a mild case of bad taste. The language
used is in some parts quite untranslatable, but we can be
sure it did not shock Hall-Stevenson, or tell him anything
he had not heard often before. The situation existing
between Sterne and his wife had been common knowledge
for several years among their friends, so that we can hardly
be aroused to Thackeray's heights of indignation by
Sterne's confession.

However, the letter is interesting on another score. The
"devil of love," he told Hall, was driving him to London,
and this, coupled with his earlier complaint of separation
from a loved one, is the clue to a minor love affair in the
city. The woman whose charms would have kept Sterne
in the city and now lured him back was probably Mrs.
Elizabeth Vesey; we can be quite sure it was not—as some-
one suggested—Kitty de Fourmantelle.

Sterne had met Mrs. Vesey through his Bluestocking
cousin-by-marriage, Mrs. Montagu. This meeting must
have taken place in June, not more than a week or two
before Sterne's departure for Coxwould. He was en-
chanted by her; he found her, he declared, in a letter written only a short time after their meeting, "graceful, & elegant & most desirable." Having struck a familiar attitude,
he went on:

But that You are sensible, and gentle and tender—&
from end to the other of you full of the sweetest tones

and modulations, requires a Connoisseur of more taste & feeling—in honest truth You are a System of harmonic Vibrations—You are the sweetest and best tuned, of all Instruments—O Lord! I would give away my other Cassoc to touch you—but in giving this last rag of my Priesthood for this pleasure you perceive I should be left naked—nay, if not quite dis-ordered:—so divine a hand as yours would presently get me into order again—but if You suppose, this would leave me, as You found me—believe me dear Lady, You are mistaken.

The field of pursuit was an old one to Sterne, and he might have forgotten to return to Coxwould. But Mrs. Vesey, who lived in London only during the winters, returned to her home in Ireland for the summer, and Sterne went back to Coxwould, to spend the summer in melancholy thought of her.

As the season drew on, he threw himself, with all his energy, into the new *Shandy,* and found it his only relief that autumn. "If God," he wrote Hall, "had not poured forth the spirit of Shandeism into me, which will not suffer me to think two moments upon any grave subject, I would, else, just now lie down and die. . . . To-morrow morning (if Heaven permit) I begin the fifth volume of *Shandy.* I care not a curse for the critics. I'll load my vehicle with what goods *he* sends me, and they may take 'em off my hands, or let them alone."

It was not until some time in August that Sterne was able to settle down to work on his book. His restlessness alone would have kept him from it; but another matter had also intervened. Sterne had hopes of going down to Cambridge for his doctor's degree, and with this in mind he had been working on the required Latin dissertation. Ten years before he had written such a *clerum* for his friend, Dean Fountayne, and in his bitter moments he sometimes resented having done the work for which another had received the honor. However, even while he was working on his own *clerum*, he doubted that he would ever actually apply for the degree, and, in fact, he never did. By August, however, he was ready for *Shandy*, and he started to work on it at his usual speed.

The influence of his summer melancholy and a new love are everywhere apparent in the third installment of *Tristram Shandy*, comprising the fifth and sixth volumes. These volumes are not, of course, entirely free from suggestiveness—(nor can we agree with Sterne's Victorian critics that a *Shandy* entirely free from suggestiveness would have represented the author at his best, any more than Rabelais free from Rabelaisian humor would have represented the Frenchman at his best). The fifth and sixth volumes were written more sensitively, with a greater display of Sterne's narrative and descriptive power than is shown in the preceding volumes. A part of this is due, no doubt, to his developing ability as a writer, but in large part these characteristics were the result of his mood. Sterne the impressionist had already been on display in the earlier volumes, but in this installment we find Sterne emerging as a master of pathos. It was the man of feeling who wrote the tender story of Lieutenant Le Fever's death. Sterne forgot to laugh as he wrote of Toby's gentle concern for the dying man:

—In a fortnight or three weeks, added my uncle Toby, smiling,—he might march.——He will never march; an' please your honour, in this world, said the corporal:—He will march; said my uncle Toby, rising up from the side of the bed, with one shoe off:— . . . . ——A-well-o'day,—do what we can for him, said Trim, maintaining his point,—the poor soul will die:——He shall not die, by G—, cried my uncle Toby.

> —The Accusing Spirit, which flew up to heaven's chancery with the oath, blushed as he gave it in;—and the Recording Angel, as he wrote it down, dropped a tear upon the word, and blotted it out for ever.

Le Fever's last moments were managed with an artistry none the less sublime. Sterne, with excellent visual power, sketched the scene of the dying man looking feebly up from his bed, while my uncle Toby, with childish simplicity, tried vainly to encourage life back into the wasted frame:

> —You shall go home directly, Le Fever, said my uncle Toby, to my house,—and we'll send for a doctor to see what's the matter,—and we'll have an apothecary,—and the corporal shall be your nurse;—and I'll be your servant, Le Fever. . . . .
> —The blood and spirits of Le Fever, which were waxing cold and slow within him, and were retreating to their last citadel, the heart—rallied back,—— the film forsook his eyes for a moment,—he looked up wishfully in my uncle Toby's face,—then cast a look upon his boy,—and that ligament, fine as it was,—was never broken.——
> Nature instantly ebbed again,—the film returned to its place,—the pulse fluttered—stopped—went on— throbbed—stopped again—moved—stopped—shall I go on?—No.

The mood of love and melancholy even tempered Sterne's satire. It is present in this installment, but it is not so sharp—it is more subtle—than in the past. In my uncle Toby's *Apologetical Oration* for the militarists the satire is so finely drawn that most of Sterne's commentators have interpreted the "oration" with a straight face. Sterne was never better than when he wrote for Toby his defense of war:

Need I be told, dear Yorick, as I was by you, in Le Fever's funeral sermon, That so soft and gentle a creature, born to love, to mercy, and kindness, as man is, was not shaped for this?—But why did you not add, Yorick,—if not by nature—that he is so by necessity?—For what is war? what is it, Yorick, when fought as ours has been, upon principles of liberty, and upon principles of honour—what is it, but the getting together of quiet and harmless people, with their swords in their hands, to keep the ambitious and the turbulent within bounds? And heaven is my witness, brother Shandy, that the pleasure I have taken in these things,—and that infinite delight, in particular, which had attended my sieges in my bowling-green, has arose within me, and I hope in the corporal too, from the consciousness we both had, that in carrying them on, we were answering the great ends of our creation.

Could Caesar have concocted more nobly a *raison d'être* for his campaigns?

Sterne did not forget his critics, who had so mercilessly flayed him for his last installment. He wrote them into his third installment as a troop of jackasses. "How they viewed and reviewed us as we passed over a rivulet at the bottom of that little valley," he wrote, "—and when we climbed over that hill and were just getting out of sight— good God! what a braying did they all set up together!" His mood led him more into paths of self-pity than vitriol, however, and in the sixth volume we find one page left blank, a page which "malice will not blacken and which ignorance cannot misrepresent."

By mid-autumn the two new volumes were finished. But a misunderstanding with Dodsley left Sterne in a quandary for a publisher. This, as well as his desire to see the lovely Mrs. Vesey, drove him Londonward earlier than usual, and he was probably in the city before the end of November. Within a few days arrangements had been made with another publishing firm, Becket and Dehondt, in the Strand, who remained Sterne's publishers to the end. Through the first weeks of December Sterne was busy with the proofs and details of publication, and on December 21, the two new volumes appeared, bearing a dedication to Lord Spencer, and a dedication of the story of Le Fever to Lady Spencer. This was the dedication to which Johnson objected because of its poor grammatical structure. The great lexicographer met Sterne for the first time at the home of Sir Joshua Reynolds, who had painted Sterne's portrait on the author's first visit to London. Sterne read to the company his dedication, and Johnson informed him flatly that "it was not English, sir." Sterne also offended Johnson by showing an indecent drawing, and the two parted unfriendly. Johnson, the moralist and lexicographer, never forgave Sterne either affront.

The price of the two volumes had been reduced from five to four shillings. This, together with the change in publishers, and a rumor that had been widely circulated, to the effect that the author of *Tristram Shandy* had died the previous summer, led Sterne to fear that his latest effort might be looked upon as merely another spurious imitation. For this reason he signed each copy of the fifth volume before it was placed on sale; however, since his signature was not widely enough known to reassure prospective purchasers, the satisfaction of Sterne's effort was confined to himself. Thus the first edition of the fifth volume exists today only with Sterne's autograph.

Since his arrival in London he had spent much time with Mrs. Vesey. Together they went to Ranelagh, and her voice charmed him in her "warm cabinet." To Mrs. Montagu, who had brought them together, he declared that never had he seen "anything so truly graceful as she is, nor had I an idea until I saw her that Grace could be so perfect in all its parts—" As usual, he was swamped with invitations to dine from the great and fashionable, and he managed to be everywhere of importance in London during the first three weeks of December. He visited Mrs. Vesey in company with Lord Bath, and talked with the old statesman in Sir Joshua Reynolds' studio, while the artist painted Lord Bath's last portrait. He was taken up by the Spencers, and lionized. He went to Mrs. Montagu's party.

In the midst of this round of gaiety, the inevitable occurred; a blood vessel again burst in his lungs, and he suffered the worst hemorrhage he had ever had. The illness which had been with him from youth now threatened him seriously, and he was warned that another winter in England would be his last. Sterne had been considering for some months a trip to the south of France, for his health's sake. In the previous summer he had asked Hall to arrange for him to accompany a young nobleman to the Continent as "bear leader"—governor. Now it appeared he must make the trip at his own expense, if he wished to live.

For several days he was confined to his rooms, and Mrs. Vesey proved a charming nurse. She came and talked to him, or played at picquet, and Sterne was touched by her devotion—or such he interpreted it. To Mrs. Montagu he recited her efforts to charm him out of his illness, and insisted that she had kept him from death's door—". . . if I had ever so great an inclination to cross the gulph, while such a woman beckoned me to stay,—I could not depart."

But, even while Sterne put a bold face on the matter, death followed more closely on his heels as he took his way through London's great houses. The French journey could now no longer be postponed. That Sterne was a practical and methodical man is shown by the preparation he made. With Mrs. Montagu he left a "Memorandum" addressed to Mrs. Sterne. It shows him a thoughtful husband and father. He listed the papers which might be sold or published in the event of his death, and indicated the disposal to be made of his estate, estimated at 1,800 pounds. He charged his wife not to leave herself dependent upon anyone's delusive promises, in case Lydia should marry. "Reserve enough for your comfort," he warned her, "—or let her wait your Death." If he died abroad, he begged his wife to remember his estranged sister Catherine, and do something for her. "We shall meet again," he concluded, and two tears dropped upon the paper and left their mute testimony to his emotion as he wrote.

At last all was ready. Finding himself short of cash, he borrowed twenty pounds from Garrick. It was Hall-Stevenson who bade him good-bye in London, and helped him into the carriage. Death had found him out, he told Eugenius in the next installment of *Shandy*.

Thou hast had a narrow escape, Tristram, said Eugenius, taking hold of my hand as I finished my story—

But there is no living, Eugenius, replied I, at this rate; for as this son of a whore has found out my lodgings—

—You call him rightly, said Eugenius,—for by sin, we are told, he entered the world—I care not which way he entered, quoth I, provided he be not in such a hurry to take me out with him—for I have forty volumes to write and forty thousand things to say and do. . . . . .—Then, by heaven! I will lead him a dance he little thinks of—for I will gallop, quoth I, without looking once behind me, to the banks of the Garonne; and if I hear him clattering at my heels—I'll scamper away to mount Vesuvius—from thence to

Joppa, and from Joppa to the world's end; where, if
he follows me, I pray God he may break his neck—
He runs more risk there, said Eugenius, than thou.

Eugenius's wit and affection brought blood into
the cheek from whence it had been some months ban-
ished—'twas a vile moment to bid adieu in; he led
me to my chaise—Allons! said I; the postboy gave a
crack with his whip—off I went like a cannon, and in
half a dozen bounds got into Dover.

Thus began Sterne's flight from death. The black ras-
cal was not to catch up with him this time. Sterne would
live to write several more of those forty volumes still unwritten.

XIV
Continental Interlude

THE next three years comprise an interlude in Sterne's life. While he recruited his health on the Continent he wrote nothing, and it is an interesting commentary on his status as a popular writer that he was able easily to regain his public acclaim in England at the end of three years.

When Hall-Stevenson and the other intimates of Sterne bade him godspeed, few expected ever to see him alive again. Sterne himself feared the worst, and death lay heavy upon him as his tears dropped upon the words to his wife, "We shall meet again." The newspapers, which were just then reprinting the affecting story of Le Fever, watched the news from abroad for word of Sterne's death, and the *Chronicle* actually printed a rumor that he had died about a month after his departure from London. This rumor of his death in Paris was widely current, and was reprinted in many newspapers throughout England. It was even said that his parishioners at Coxwould, who had entertained the highest respect for him, went into mourning upon hearing the false account.

But Sterne himself, like a later humorist, was able to report that the rumor of his death had been greatly exaggerated. How close death had been, only Sterne alone knew. On the boat from Dover he had lain in his cabin, too sick to get up, and sure that now he would meet death "full in the face." The next morning he left Calais by post for Paris, going through Boulogne, Montreuil, and Amiens. At last, arriving in Paris in mid-January, he considered an immediate departure for the south of France. His physicians had warned him that his only chance to live through the winter would be to seek this easier climate. Despite their consultations, there was nothing they could do for him, and they had given him up as hopeless of recovery.

However, even the shadow of death could not completely alter Sterne. Within two weeks after his arrival in Paris, he was caught up in a whirl of dinners, theatre parties, and friendships to rival the best that London had ever done for him. His doctors, amazed at this apparent return from the dead, advised him that a trip to the south was no longer necessary, and by the time the London newspapers were reporting the author's death, Sterne was making his report to Garrick with all the life and gaiety of his London Shandeism:

> Well! here I am, my friend, as much improved in my health, for the time, as ever your friendship could wish, or, at least, your faith give credit to.—By the bye, I am somewhat worse in my intellectuals; for my head is turned round with what I see, and the unexpected honors I have met with here. Tristram was almost as much known here as in London, at least among your men of condition and learning, and has got me introduced into so many circles ('tis *comme à Londres.*) I have just now a fortnight's dinners and suppers upon my hands.

Because of the hostilities between England and France, travelers found it difficult to secure passports, and Sterne had been forced to come away without one. In France he applied to the proper authorities, and got one without trouble, although he was assured that "Had it been for any one but the king's jester, I could not have got it these two hours." Sterne's fame had traveled before him, and his new Parisian friends offered to guarantee his conduct in France. Among these was the Baron d'Holbach, whom Sterne described as "one of the most leârned noblemen here, the great protector of wits, and of the *Scavans,* who are no wits;—keeps open house three dâys a week." The Baron became attached to the humorist, and Sterne spent many hours in his company. He fell in, also, with the small colony of English fashionables resident in Paris. With Sir George Macartney, the future stâtesman, and young Stephen Fox, he struck up a warm friendship. They took Sterne to Versailles and introduced him to Titon, an art patron known to Garrick. At the theatre he saw Clairon in *Iphigene,* and he wrote enthusiastically to Garrick, "—would to God you had one or two like her! What a luxury, to see you with one of such powêrs in the same interesting scene!" He saw *The Frenchman in London,* "in which Preville is to send us home to supper all happy."

But he soon tired of Paris. He declared he could not abide the hypocrisies of the Parisian etiquette. He met no woman here, he told Garrick, to compare with Mrs. Garrick, who had quite captivated him in London. At the theatre there was nothing "here which gives the nerves so smart a blow as those great characters in the hands of Garrick!" He tired of the comic opera and endless discussions of the Jesuits, who were just then out of favor. The French Comedy he found tiring, for they acted only tragedies, and he could not "bear preaching." He wrote, "There is a tragedy to be damned to-night; peace be with it, and the gentle brain which made it!" To Garrick Sterne sent a copy of Diderot's *The Natural Son;* with the fear that Garrick would find it unacceptable, he neverthe-

less sent it to him to read. He assured Garrick that Paris
was looking forward to the actor's visit, as soon as peace
between the two countries permitted.

News came from Coxwould that Lydia, who had suffered from childhood with asthma, was worse. Sterne
planned to bring Mrs. Sterne and Lydia to France and take
a house in the south, where they might live together
through the following winter. He applied to the authorities for permission to have them join him, and he decided
if this was impossible to return to England in the late
spring. His application was granted, and Sterne looked
forward to a reunion with his family—a reunion which had
seemed almost impossible a few months earlier.

In the preparations which Sterne made for their comfort
on the journey, he reveals again the methodical man and
the loving husband and father. Despite the breach between him and his wife, he was honestly glad of the approaching reunion, and he looked forward with keen anticipation to seeing his Lydia again. Only a man who has
been snatched from the brink of almost certain death
could appreciate what emotions Sterne felt as he wrote his
wife and daughter instructions for their voyage. With almost every mail post he thought of new instructions, or he
was besieged by new fears for their comfort:

For God's sake, rise early and gallop away in the
cool;—and always see that you have not forgot your
baggage in changing post-chaises.—You will find good
tea upon the road from York to Dover;—only bring a
little to carry you from Calais to Paris.—Give the
custom-house officers what I told you;—at Calais give
more, if you have much Scotch snuff;—but as tobacco
is good here, you had best bring a Scotch-mill and
make it yourself; that is, order your valet to manufac-
ture it;—'twill keep him out of mischief.—I would ad-
vise you to take three days in coming up, for fear of

heating yourselves.—See that they do not give you a bad vehicle, when a better is in the yard; but you will look sharp.—Drink small Rhenish, to keep you cool (that is, if you like it). Live well, and deny yourselves nothing your hearts wish. So God in Heaven prosper and go along with you!—kiss my Lydia, and believe me both affectionately, yours—

Up to the very last moment he thought of new devices for their comfort, new precautions they must take in traveling—and every few days a new letter went out to Yorkshire. These letters reveal Sterne in a simple, unaffected light—they are full of small talk and a genuine concern for his family. These letters could hardly find their peer in the most sincere effusions of the most faithful husbands; though they were devoid of sentiment, they surprise an honesty of affection which makes them the truest love-letters Sterne ever wrote. Merely another paradox of Sterne's character—the man is ever to be discovered in these paradoxes.

At last mother and daughter set out. They were to travel in France in a chaise Sterne had bought for them from a gentleman, at a great bargain. His last letter of instructions caught them just as they were "upon the wing." He concluded it, "—Dear Bess, I have a thousand wishes; but have a hope for every one of them;—you shall chant the same *jubilate,* my dears: so God bless you!" There were legal matters to attend to in York: Croft was given power of attorney to act for Sterne in matters regarding his property. Sterne wrote to the Archbishop and secured an extended leave of absence. Mrs. Sterne went to Becket, the publisher, and received from him a draft on his Paris banker for the amount due Sterne. Sterne had hoped Becket might be induced to take over the copies of the third *Shandy* still unsold—about 4,000 of them—and even purchase the copyright. But Becket declined these risks, and paid only Sterne's share of the copies already sold. With all these things to attend to, it was well on toward the end of June before the two turned their faces toward France. At Dover they stopped, on Sterne's instructions, at the Cross Keys Inn, and at Calais at the Lyon D'Argent. Because of the heat they traveled very slowly, and arrived in Paris on the eighth of July.

In the meantime, Sterne's condition had taken a turn for the worse. Early in the spring, following a trip to Versailles on his wife's behalf, he had fallen ill. But he was soon up and around, continuing his "shandying about" with all his usual energy. This, together with his constant worries over his wife's comfort and the Paris heat—"as hot as Nebuchadnezzar's oven"—resulted in another hemorrhage of the lungs. "About a week or ten days before my wife arrived in Paris," he reported to John Hall-Stevenson in a letter, "I had the same accident I had at Cambridge, of breaking a vessel in my lungs. It happened in the night,—and I bled the bed full; and finding in the morning I was likely to bleed to death, I sent immediately for a surgeon to bleed me at both arms:—this saved me; and with lying speechless three days, I recovered upon my back in bed; the breach healed, and, in a week after, I got out."

He was up in time to welcome his wife and daughter to Paris. He was happy to see his wife again, although he predicted that "a year will tire us all out, I trow." As for Lydia, he was delighted with her. He found her unaffected, and declared he wished "she may ever remain a child of Nature:—I hate children of Art." His recent illness, despite the casualness with which he dismissed it, had alarmed Sterne, and this, together with the heat, caused him to decide on immediate departure for the south. He had taken a large house at Toulouse, which

he described as "elegant beyond anything I look'd for."
It was built, he wrote his banker, Foley, in Paris, "in the
form of a hotel, with a pretty court towards the town;—
and behind, the best garden in Toulouse, laid out in ser-
pentine walks; and so large, that the company in our quarter usually come to walk there in the evening, for which
they have my consent:—'the more the merrier.' The house
consists of a good *salle à manger* above stairs, joining to
the very great *salle à compagnie* as large as the Baron
d'Holbach's; three handsome bed chambers, with dressing
rooms to them;—below stairs, two very good rooms for
myself; one to study in, the other to see company.—I have
moreover cellars round the court, and all other offices."
The landlord also allowed the Sternes the use of a country house two miles out from the town, and agreed to care
for the gardens. For all this Sterne was to pay only thirty
pounds a year! Little wonder he felt like a king in his
new situation.

The trip from Paris to Toulouse consumed some three
weeks. It was so hot on the road that Sterne assured Foley
he had not seen a cloud in the sky half as broad as a small
coin. "We were toasted, roasted, grill'd, stew'd, and car-
bonaded on one side or other all the way." At night they
were bedeviled by vermin in the untidy inns. And, to
make matters worse, the carriage broke down just outside
of Lyons. A cart was brought for the baggage, and the
three walked along behind it into the city.

As they entered the city, a chaise-vamper called to them,
asking if they wished to have the carriage repaired, or
would sell it. Sterne sold his chaise, and decided to travel
by boat to Avignon. After a night spent in Lyons, he
awoke early to see the sights of the city before taking the
noon boat. But—according to the account in *Tristram
Shandy*—he suddenly missed his notebook, and recollected

that he had left it in the carriage. He returned to the chaise-vamper's house and found that the tradesman's wife had twisted the sheets of his notes to use as curling papers. With many apologies she untwisted them from her hair and handed the sheets back to him, one by one. So much for the anecdote. At any rate, the notes were recovered, and formed the basis for the seventh volume of *Shandy*. If the incident was not literally true, its fabrication is delightful; it adds a grotesque Shandaic touch of the sort that Sterne so loved.

From Avignon, Sterne sent his wife and Lydia on by stagecoach, while he rode behind on a mule, stopping to talk to peasants along the way. He discussed with a drum-maker the intricacies of his trade, walked with a couple of Franciscans, and bought a basket of Provence figs from an old crone for four *sous*. Everything interested Sterne, and he studied the stream of humanity upon the road—"arresting all kinds of beggars, pilgrims, fiddlers, friars—not passing by a woman in a mulberry-tree without commending her legs, and tempting her into conversation with a pinch of snuff. . . . I am confident we could have passed through Pall-Mall, or St. James's Street for a month together, with fewer adventures—and seen less of human nature."

But the worst had not yet come. Somewhere near Beaucaire, the chaise carrying Mrs. Sterne and Lydia again broke down, the hind wheel breaking into "ten thousand pieces." The two postilions refused to go for aid, blubbering helplessly.

"Nothing can be done," they wept dolefully.

"By heaven," Sterne said, and began to peel off his coat, "something shall be done, for I'll thrash you both within an inch of your lives,—and then make you each take a horse and ride like two devils to the next post for a cart to carry my baggage, and a wheel to carry ourselves."

They waited for five hours on the dusty road, in the heat of the sun, until relief arrived. Peasants, on their way to the fair at Beaucaire, stopped to chat and sympathize with them.

At last the long journey was over, and the travelers arrived in Toulouse early in August. Sterne was delighted with the beautiful city, and especially with the house he had engaged. Near the Sternes lived the family of William Hewitt, and Hewitt was Sterne's companion through the remainder of the summer and autumn. The two families often dined together. Sterne liked his summer house, especially the pavilion attached to it, which he called "Pringello Pavilion," in honor of the unidentified architect of the Demoniacs.

Soon after the Sternes settled in Toulouse an epidemic spread through the city, which Sterne wrote "killed hundreds about me." Ever a prey to disease, Sterne fell ill, and for six weeks he hovered again on the brink of death. He allowed himself to be treated by the physicians, whom he declared to be "the errantest charlatans in Europe, or the most ignorant of all pretending fools." Seeing himself fail under their ministrations, he "withdrew what was left of me out of their hands, and recommended my affair entirely to Dame Nature: she (dear goddess)," he wrote Hall-Stevenson, "has saved me in fifty different pinching bouts; and I begin to have a kind of enthusiasm now in her favor, and in my own, that one or two more escapes will make me believe I shall leave you all at last by translation, and not by fair death."

But by late October, Sterne was "stout and foolish again as a happy man can wish." He began to work on the next installment of *Tristram Shandy*, hoping no doubt to complete it in time for publication that winter. He busied himself "playing the fool with my uncle Toby, whom I have got soused over head and ears in love." However, other matters intervened, and my uncle Toby's courtship of the Widow Wadman was not destined to be given to the public that year, nor the next.

With the approach of winter, the social life of Toulouse became gayer. The English colony was augmented, and Sterne found other things to do. My uncle Toby's amours were laid away in the study. The English hibernating in Toulouse were pleasantly surprised to find so famous a jester in their midst, and Sterne, ever ready for gaiety, proposed that they form a company to act plays for their own amusement. They performed *The Busybody*, with a *"grand orchestra"*; this was followed by a performance of *The Journey to London*, which with the alteration of a few lines became *The Journey to Toulouse*. Thus the winter passed, with Sterne outwardly as gay as he was in London.

But there were many vexations beneath the surface. Throughout the winter he was troubled by money matters. Although he estimated his entire expense at Toulouse at about two hundred and fifty pounds a year, his income was hardly sufficient. Since Mrs. Sterne's settlement with Becket, the publisher had sold less than two hundred additional sets of the *Shandy* installment. Several times that winter Sterne was forced to apply to his banker, Foley, in Paris, for advances, with the assurance that he had "no more than half a dozen guineas in his pocket"—and again, "I have not five *Louis* to vapor with in this land of coxcombs." He had been unable to go on with the next installment and for the first time in four years, London was without its new volumes of *Tristram* that winter. Added to his money worries was the matter of his constantly failing health. Despite his gaiety, he had not really mended properly in Toulouse. The climate had not

agreed with him, any more than the experiments of his
Toulouse physicians, and by spring he was advised to try
the waters of Bagnères, in the Pyrenees.

Sterne addressed another letter to the Archbishop, tac-
itly requesting an extension of his leave. He feared,
Sterne told his superior, that he should never preach again.
The request granted, Sterne took his family in June to
Bagnères. However, the waters benefited him little, and
the thin mountain air of the Pyrenees proved disastrous
to his lungs. Sterne had planned also to go to Spain for
a week, "—which is enough for a fertile brain to write a
volume upon.—When I write the history of my travels—"
Whether he actually went to Spain is uncertain, although
we can assume that he did not. The family remained
some two months in Bagnères, instead of the three months
on which Sterne had originally planned. They returned
first to Toulouse, where a draft from Foley for 1,500 livres
awaited Sterne. Thus fortified, the Sternes left Toulouse
and traveled about for several weeks, visiting Montpelier,
Aix, and Marseilles. At last they decided upon Montpelier as the place to spend the winter, despite Sterne's
discovery that living expenses were higher here than in
Toulouse.

The Sternes settled in Montpelier for the winter on
about the first of October. Although they had to forego
the luxury of a big house such as they had occupied at
Toulouse, they were comfortable enough in Montpelier.
The winter was in many ways a repetition of the previous
one. The Sternes mingled with the small English colony,
and the Hewitts had come from Toulouse for the winter.
There were friendly gatherings for dinner and parties for
the theatre—to hear the concerts or see the plays performed
by a traveling company at the *Comédie*.

There is some conjecture as to whether Sterne met Smollett, the novelist, here. Smollett, whose magazine had attacked Sterne viciously in its reviews of *Shandy*, came to Montpelier in November to consult a famous physician on his asthma. The novelist was greeted by members of the English colony, and later remembered a conversation with Mrs. Sterne. But if a meeting between Sterne and Smollett occurred, neither ever mentioned it, although Sterne retaliated for the attacks of the *Critical Review* by caricaturing the embittered novelist in *A Sentimental Journey* as Smelfungus the traveler.

Montpelier turned out to be even worse for Sterne's health than Toulouse had been. After some treatments with bouillons, lasting a month, his physicians advised him that to remain in Montpelier would be fatal. "And why, good people, were you not kind enough to tell me this sooner?" Sterne commented. He began to make his plans to return to England. Again this winter there had been no new installment of his book, and he was anxious to "lay a tax" upon his public. He would have wished to return by way of Belgium and Holland, but the thought of spending some time with his friends attracted him again to Paris. Mrs. Sterne refused to return to England, pleading the cause of her own and Lydia's health. Sterne consented with misgivings to their remaining in France. He foresaw "a tear at parting with my little slut"—and he prepared to return to England alone.

Early in March Sterne left Montpelier for Paris. Although he had intended to spend only a few weeks in Paris, the few weeks, as usual, lengthened into two months or more. Among Sterne's friends here were Stephen Fox, John Wilkes, the politician who had been removed from the House of Commons, and Lawson Trotter, John Hall-Stevenson's Jacobite uncle who had lived in exile since the uprising of 1745. Sterne lived with his friend, M. Tollot, in the Quartier St. Honoré. The flow of travel between England and France, which had waned with the war, had once again set in, and the English colony in Paris was much larger than when Sterne had last been in the city two years before. The company was gay and the weeks passed pleasantly, with dinners and theatres, much as in London.

Sterne was honored with an invitation to deliver a sermon before the Ambassador. Although he had declared he should never preach again, he ascended the pulpit of the little church in the Faubourg St. Honoré. We can imagine the gathering Sterne must have attracted on the occasion—all the English, divided at home but companions in exile; fashionable and literary Parisians, curious to hear the jester Yorick in a role that seemed hardly to fit him. The little chapel was filled to capacity as Sterne began his sermon; there was, he declared in a letter to Lydia, "a concourse of all nations, and religions too." His subject dealt with Hezekiah, who incurred the displeasure of Isaiah for showing the royal treasures to the Babylonian ambassadors, on the text, *And he said, What have they seen in thine house? And Hezekiah answered, All the things that are in mine house have they seen: there is nothing among all my treasures that I have not showed them.* A strange text to discuss before the ambassador to a recently hostile nation, and Sterne may have been something less than naive in the choice! Sterne was honored that evening at a dinner, and the historian Hume, who was present, twitted Sterne gently on his sermon.

Yorick, who must be always the philanderer, could hardly have remained in Paris two months without an *affaire d'amour,* and this visit was no exception. The woman is unidentified, but Sterne's combustible heart caught fire easily. In a letter to Hall-Stevenson he confessed that the affair had begun within a few days after his arrival in Paris:

> . . . . I have been for eight weeks smitten with the tenderest passion that ever tender wight underwent. I wish, dear cosin, thou couldest conceive (perhaps thou can'st without my wishing it) how deliciously I canter'd away with it the first month, two up, two down, always upon my hânches along the streets from my hotel to hers, at first once—then twice, then three times a day, till at length I was within an ace of setting up my hobby horse in her stall for good and all. I might as well considering how the enemies of the Lord have blasphemed thereupon; the last three weeks we were every hour upon the doleful ditty of parting—and thou mayest conceive, dear cousin, how it alter'd my gaite and air—for I went and came like any louden'd earl, and did nothing but mix tears, and *jouer des sentiments* with her from sun-rising even to the setting of the same. . . .

But at last, about the middle of May, the sentimental little romance was over; the object of it left Paris for the south of France, and Sterne could turn his eyes again toward England. While he was preparing to leave France, he again broke a vessel in his lungs and suffered another serious hemorrhage. But he was soon up and ready for the crossing to his green hills of Coxwould.

Before Sterne left Paris, his thoughts turned again to Lydia, whom he was leaving among people whose manners and influence he sometimes deplored. He sent his daughter books and magazines—he hoped for her edification—and a guitar for her musical development. Although she dabbled in art, her father assured her she had no talent for it, and advised her to give it up. But chiefly he stressed a bit of fatherly advice on a subject which disturbed him. "I hope you have not forgot my last request," he wrote, "to make no friendships with the French women;—not that

I think ill of them all; but sometimes women of the best principles are the most *insinuating;*—nay, I am so jealous of you, that I should be miserable to see you had the least grain of coquetry in your composition."

To the last, he disliked leaving Lydia in France. But Mrs. Sterne was adamant, and Sterne could not deny anything which might be for his daughter's health. So, reconciled again to parting, he left Paris toward the end of May and saw the cliffs of Dover before him, for the first time in two and a half years.

XV

The Jester and the Lady

ONCE more across the channel, Sterne could look back on his French interlude with a great deal of satisfaction. His reception in Paris had been more than he had a right to expect, for *Tristram Shandy* had not yet been translated into French, and Sterne's eccentricities of language and syntax made an understanding of the English version by the French extremely difficult. Voltaire, among others, read the English version and had high praise for it, while many of the French journals discussed the volumes at length and gave résumés of *Shandy*. Thus Sterne came to the French not entirely unknown, and, as in London, his appearance in the salons was enhanced by the high patronage under which he traveled. In Paris he frequented the salon of the Baron d'Holbach, which numbered in its group many of the leading literary men and philosophers of the time. Voltaire and Diderot were among them, and Sterne struck up an intimacy with the latter.

However, of the friends Sterne made in France, from our point of view Suard ranks as the most important. This was Jean Baptiste Suard, who wrote of Sterne in the *Gazette Littéraire*. Perhaps Suard was thinking of writing Sterne's biography; at any rate the young man became very intimate with Sterne and observed him as he made

his way through the fashionable circles of Paris.   Later
both Suard and his wife wrote of Sterne, and Suard's impressions serve to throw much light on Sterne's character
and manners at the time.   Suard was struck with Sterne's
ability to adapt himself to the manners of the country,
often outdoing the French in the practice of the polite etiquette for which they were famed; yet at the same time
he saw and appreciated in Sterne a critical frankness.
Sterne evidently thought highly of the young journalist,
for he revealed himself to the young man in a frank self-
analysis.   Aside from his native creative ability, Sterne
declared his works indebted to his reading of the Old and
New Testaments and the philosophy of Locke.

Other testimony of Sterne's impressions on Paris is to
be found in a letter from Tollot, Sterne's host during the
second visit to Paris, addressed to Hall-Stevenson.   Professor Cross quotes from this letter, "I sometimes envy
the happy disposition of our friend Mr. Sterne.   Everything assumes the color of the rose for that happy mortal;
and what appears to others dark and gloomy, presents to
him only a blithe and merry aspect.   His only pursuit is
pleasure; but he is not like most others who do not know
how to enjoy pleasure when it is within their grasp; for
he drinks the bowl to the last drop and still his thirst is
unquenched."   Alas! poor Yorick.   A long struggle against
poverty and ill health made him a hedonist, and the acclaim of the public made him a clown.   But Paris saw
many virtues beneath the jester's cloak that London seems
to have overlooked.

Sterne did not return directly to Coxwould.   He arrived
in London about the first of June, and spent the remainder
of the month in the city.   Few of his friends were in London at the time, and the only notable event of this month
in the city was the painting of a new portrait of him by

Reynolds. Tiring of the city, Sterne left toward the end of the month, but even then he did not go directly to Coxwould. Instead he stopped in York, remaining about two months, or at least until the end of the races in August. Here he met several of his friends, including Hall-Stevenson, who had a horse running. Toward the end of August he felt it was time to return to his parsonage and a new installment of *Tristram Shandy*. Accordingly he returned to Coxwould, but a sojourn in the lonely parsonage was not to his mood, and within a week or two after his arrival, he was writing to Hall-Stevenson:

> Now, my dear, dear Anthony—I do not think a week or ten days playing the good fellow (at this very time) at Scarborough so abominable a thing—but if a man could get there cleverly. . . . I have no one to consult in this affair:—therefore, as a man may do worse things, the English of all which is this,—That I am going to leave a few poor sheep here in the wilderness for fourteen days;—and, from pride and naughtiness of heart, to go and see what is doing at Scarborough,—steadfastly meaning afterwards to lead a new life and strengthen my faith.

He had already begun again on *Shandy*, "not rapidly, but well enough." However, "there is no sitting and cudgeling one's brains while the sun shines bright," he declared philosophically; and packing his bags, he was off again for Scarborough, to drink the waters and attend the races in company with the Earl of Shelburne and the Marquis of Granby. Hall-Stevenson was at Harrogate and did not join the company.

By the end of September, Sterne was through "playing the good fellow." Feeling himself somewhat improved in health through drinking the waters at Scarborough, he returned to Coxwould, determined to complete his two volumes of *Shandy* by the middle of November. There was good reason for a new installment by now; Mrs. Sterne's expenses were greater than Sterne had anticipated. Although he had left with her a hundred pounds on his departure in the spring, he had found it necessary to draw on Foley for embarrassingly large amounts to cover his wife's extravagance. However, all did not run well with my uncle Toby's wooing of the Widow Wadman. Sterne was distracted by a visit from two charming young ladies, who kept him from his work; and he had a more serious distraction when the parsonage at Sutton was burned to the ground through the carelessness of his curate, Marmaduke Collier. Although the rebuilding of the house would mean a serious financial burden on Sterne, he met the news of this accident with philosophical calm. The curate, fearing Sterne's anger, had fled with his wife and child; but Sterne found them, gave them a place in his house at Coxwould until other quarters could be provided for them, and treated them with greatest kindness. His loss through the man's carelessness was around three hundred pounds, but he could not find it in his heart to be harsh. "Heavens! how little did he know of me," Sterne declared, "to suppose I was among the number of those wretches that heap misfortune upon misfortune—and when the load is almost insupportable, still to add to the weight! God, who reads my heart, knows it to be true—that I wish rather to share, than to encrease the burthen of the miserable—"

With all this, Sterne's writing suffered. By November he had completed only a single small volume, and he faced the prospect of another winter without revenues from his books. But Sterne was always ingenious in these matters. He shifted the seventh volume, dealing with my uncle Toby's amours, to the position of the eighth. Then, rewriting the notes on his travels as a tour made by Tristram

Shandy, he substituted that as the seventh volume. Carrying the satirical manner through his account of the French journey, he described "as odd a tour through France as ever was projected or executed by traveler, or travel-writer, since the world began.—'Tis a laughing, good-tempered satire," he wrote Foley in Paris, "against travelling (as *puppies* travel)—"

In December Sterne was again ready for the old London campaign. There were several factors to be overcome this year: London had almost forgotten *Tristram Shandy* in the three years of Sterne's absence, and the sale of the previous volumes had fallen to almost nothing. In addition, the rumors of Sterne's death had persisted long and tenaciously. Yet, in spite of this, Sterne made his way back into favor with almost miraculous ease. The volumes appeared late in January, 1765, and while the critics set up their impotent howling, the public flocked to pay the tax Sterne had levied. While the satire on those travelers who go about with their noses buried in guidebooks was not generally appreciated, the public was quite captivated by my uncle Toby's whimsical attempt at lovemaking. To their credit, it must be admitted that the critics saw through the makeshift of the volume of travels, and resented Sterne's attempts to "cheat" the public. Nevertheless, there are delightful things in the seventh volume, and although a volume of travels might have been considered an unwarranted digression in the midst of what was purportedly a novel, Sterne may easily be forgiven. In France the installment found a more appreciative hearing among the critics.

However, in spite of the critics, Sterne had little difficulty in getting back into the good graces of the bookbuyers. So successful was the fourth installment that almost as soon as it was off the press Sterne was planning another "tax" on the public. He proposed to issue two more volumes of sermons, for which he would receive advance subscriptions. By the middle of March, fashionable England had responded so generously that Sterne was able to write Garrick in Paris, "It goes into the world with a prancing list *de toute la noblesse;* which will bring me in three hundred pounds, exclusive of the sale of the copy;— so that, with all the contempt of money which *ma façon de penser* has ever impressed on me, I shall be rich in spite of myself. . . ."

The old round of dinners and activities, which had never failed Sterne since the first time he came to London, set in again. Through the winter and early spring he made his way through the houses of the great—but this time with more than a little method. For wherever he went, Sterne added a name to his "prancing list." Noblemen, churchmen, leaders of fashion, patrons of the arts— all shortly found their way into Sterne's account book, to be listed at the head of the volumes which Becket expected to issue the following autumn. Sterne wrote letters to his friends, requesting their aid in securing subscriptions; "——'tis but a crown for sixteen sermons—Dog cheap! but I am in quest of honour, not money," his Shandean appeal went out.

Some time in March Sterne became ill, and left London for the resort of Bath. Here he was much in the company of Lord Cunningham, the Irish peer, at whose house Sterne met several Irish ladies. Among them was the Mrs. Vesey who had earlier captivated the fickle Yorick, and Mrs. Moor, with whom Sterne corresponded. Mrs. Scott, a sister of Mrs. Montagu, was also at Bath, and Sterne spent many hours in her house. The author also met Gainsborough here, and is said to have sat for a portrait.

In April Sterne returned to London much refreshed. The Garricks returned from the Continent and Sterne visited them in their Hampton house. For Mrs. Garrick—the gracious Violette—he had always had the highest admiration, and the actor, despite a minor misunderstanding, remained his friend always. Garrick was always outspoken with his friend, and an anecdote has come down to indicate the freedom with which he criticized Sterne. The actor, whose own marriage was a paragon of success, denounced men who were unfaithful to their wives, and Sterne agreed. As one version has it, Sterne declared that a man who ill-treats his wife deserves to have his house burnt over his head. Garrick looked at him and said calmly, "Then it is fortunate for you, Sterne, that you live in lodgings."

Before Sterne left London that spring he engaged his heart once more in one of those foolish flirtations. This time the object of his amorous attentions was the young Lady Percy, who later figured in a divorce scandal. All that we have of this affair is a single letter, written by Sterne soon after he met her. Going out early to dine one afternoon, he stopped at the Mount Coffee House, in Mount Street, near Lady Percy's house. In his pocket was a ticket for an entertainment that evening, but the thought of it bored him. Into his mind crept the fresh young charms of the girl; ever the pawn of impulse, Sterne asked for paper and inkhorn, and on the spur of the moment concocted one of the most indiscreet letters ever written by a man tortured by love. Yet there was something less than torture in Sterne's heart, for he could still punctuate his raptures with Shandean phrases. "Oh my dear lady—" he protested, "what a dishclout of a soul hast thou made of me? I think, by the bye, this is a little too famil-

iar an introduction, for so unfamiliar a situation as I stand
in with you—" He avowed himself lost and helpless in
the power of her charms:

> Would not any man in his senses run diametrically
> from you—and as far as his legs would carry him,
> rather than thus causelessly, foolishly, and foolhardily
> expose himself afresh—and afresh, where his heart
> and his reason tells him he shall be sure to come off
> loser, if not totally undone? Why would you tell me
> you would be glad to see me? Does it give you pleas-
> ure to make me more unhappy—or does it add to your
> triumph, that your eyes and lips have turned a man
> into a fool, whom the rest of the town is courting
> as a wit? I am a fool—the weakest, the most ductile,
> the most tender fool that ever woman tried the weak-
> ness of—and the most unsettled in my purposes and
> resolutions of recovering my right mind.

He was going to the home of a friend in Wigmore-street
to dine, and would remain there until seven. He begged
her to send him word that she was alone that evening and
would receive him. "If I hear nothing by that time, I
shall conclude you are better disposed of—and shall take
a sorry hack, and sorrily jog on to the play. Curse on the
word. I know nothing but sorrow—except this one thing,
that I love you (perhaps foolishly, but) most sincerely . . ."
Did Sterne send the letter? And did the fire receive the
moth? It would be a coquette with a heart of stone who
could refuse such an appeal, and romantically we are inclined to hope that Sterne spent that evening within happy
view of the eyes that had so charmed him. But the moralists, beginning with Thackeray, have read such horrors
into this minor indiscretion, that we must stifle the romantic impulse and hope that Sterne "jogged sorrily on to
the play."

XVI

Sentimental Journey

FOR some reason Sterne tired of London earlier that
year than was usual with him. Perhaps it was the moodi-
ness of ill health, or he may have hoped to prepare his
sermons for early publication, with a view to a return to
the Continent. At any rate, by the first or second week in
May he had left the city and was hastening home to Coxwould. He met John Hall-Stevenson in York, and during
his visit with the master of Crazy Castle, he again suffered
a hemorrhage of the lungs. This dangerous symptom had
recurred with alarming frequency in recent months, and
despite a bold front, Sterne was worried. That summer
we find him resting at Coxwould, corresponding with his
friends, working over his sermons. It was a pleasant existence, as he described it to his friend, Mrs. Meadows, trying
to lure her out to Coxwould for a visit: "I will give you a
roast fowl for your dinner, and a clean table-cloth every
day—and tell you a story by way of desert;—in the heat of
the day we will sit in the shade—and in the evening the
fairest of all the milk-maids who pass by my gate, shall
weave a garland for you."

In his letters we find Sterne exhibiting many moods.
He was gaily philosophical as he advised his friend Woodhouse on love: "I am glad that you are in love;—'twill cure
the spleen, at least, which has a bad effect on both man

and woman.—I myself must ever have some Dulcinea in my head; it harmonizes the soul;—and in those cases I first endeavour to make the lady believe so; or rather, I begin first to make myself believe that I am in love;—but I carry on my affairs quite in the French way, sentimentally,— *L'amour* (say they) *n'est rien sans sentiment.*" He was angry—although amused—at a letter from an old French gentleman who had fallen in love with Lydia and wrote to ask how large a fortune Sterne was prepared to settle on his daughter. As he retailed the account to Woodhouse, he replied, "Sir, I shall give her ten thousand pounds the day of marriage. My calculation is as follows: —She is not eighteen, you are sixty-two;—there goes five thousand pounds:—then, Sir, you at least think her not ugly; she has many accomplishments,—speaks Italian, French, plays upon the guitar; and as I fear you play upon no instrument whatever, I think you will be happy to take her at my terms; for here finishes the account of the ten thousand pounds." The chagrined suitor accepted this rebuff and made no further protestations of his love.

Occasionally Sterne left Coxwould for a visit to York. At the races in August he made the acquaintance of Elizabeth Graeme, who later figured in the attempt of the British government to seek retraction of the American Declaration of Independence. As tradition has it, she was with some friends at the races, and when the wagers were being made, she selected a small, lightly favored horse. Her friends in surprise asked why, and she answered, "The race is not always to the swift, nor the battle to the strong." Sterne, who was standing by, heard the remark, and asked to be presented to her.

By early autumn the list of subscribers to the sermons was complete, numbering six hundred ninety-three names. From the Duke and Duchess of Ancaster, to Sir Thomas

Whitmore, K.C., the list could almost pass for a roll of the important men and women of England. Many French names are to be found on the list, including Diderot and Voltaire. Sterne's friends were all there—Stephen Croft, Garrick, Foley, Fox, the Marquis of Granby, the Earl of Fauconberg. It was indeed a proud assembly that welcomed the new *Sermons of Yorick* into the world of books. The two volumes made their appearance in January, 1766, later than had originally been planned. They contained only twelve sermons, instead of sixteen, and, as in the first two volumes, Sterne again inserted an additional title-page for the squeamish ones who resented seeing the name Yorick on sermons.

However, Sterne himself was not in London when the sermons were published. For the first time since the original installment of *Shandy,* his writings went through the press without his personal supervision. Sterne had come to London early in October. All the necessary arrangements were made, and Sterne departed for the Continent, leaving behind him a credit of six hundred pounds for his use in traveling. When the sermons were delivered to the subscribers, Sterne was in Rome.

Leaving London only a few days after his arrival from Coxwould, Sterne traveled by packet boat to Calais. Here he rested at the new Hotel d'Angleterre, built by Monsieur Dessein, who had come up from waiter to innkeeper. This Monsieur Dessein turned out to be a very clever business man, and he cashed in later on Sterne's brief patronage. The original hotel was burned down in 1770, but Dessein rebuilt, and fitted up a *Sterne Chamber,* where many favored travelers slept, under the fond belief they were resting where Sterne himself had sat. Sterne immortalized the innkeeper in *A Sentimental Journey,* the unfinished account of this last tour.

How much of Sterne's romantic account in *A Sentimental Journey* is a true narrative of his adventures in France? Much of it, his commentators have often assumed, and in telling the story of his Continental tour they have merely rewritten the fragment which Sterne published before his death. One wishes the account were true, for there are pretty pictures: the exchange of snuff boxes with the Franciscan monk; an adventure in Dessein's inn yard with a mysterious lady in distress, who allowed the sentimental traveler to kiss her gloved hand; the grisette in the Paris shop, who was amused when he counted her pulse beats. Sterne stopped to lament over a dead ass on the road to Nampont. At Amiens he again encountered the mysterious lady of Dessein's inn yard, and exchanged letters with her. In Paris he learned from a beggar the potency of flattery, and saw it work miracles on feminine hearts. At Moulines he met again poor Maria of the final volume of *Shandy,* whose heart had been broken by love and who now sat on the hillside and played mad music on her harp. But there are too many indications that *A Sentimental Journey* wrote itself out of Sterne's fancies, rather than his experiences. Another fact too long overlooked is that Sterne wrote *A Sentimental Journey* after he had met and fallen in love with Eliza Draper. Although certain parts of the book were based on his experiences, all of it was colored by a sentimental attachment which did not yet exist at the time of this tour and therefore could not have colored his actual experiences. The book is a record of its author's emotions at the time he wrote it, and any attempt to apply these emotions retroactively is a serious error in interpretation. As for the events he wrote about, some of them occurred on Sterne's first visit to France—as in the instance of the difficulties over his passport. Others were reworked from incidents told him by friends—as in *The Case of Delicacy,* which forms the last chapter in the book. A few no doubt were based on the actual experiences of his "sentimental journey."

Since this work represents the flowering of Sterne's "sentimentality," this would appear to be an opportune point at which to examine the elements of which his sentiment was composed. To Sterne the word "sentimental" had none of the derogatory connotations of the maudlin and bathetic that it generally has today. His first use of the word is to be found in a letter to his fiancée, and he later explained his concept of it in a letter to a friend. Sterne saw his writing as a frame, a "show box," in which he could present a series of touchingly pathetic tableaux. He invited his readers to "take a peep" into his show box, to mingle their tears with his in a thrillingly delicious orgy of emotion—always on an intellectual level—that would leave the *feelings* shaken and the *soul* untouched. Even when he professed himself the most moved by his pictures, he was actually the master of his emotion, playing upon it as on a keyboard, interpolating a wistful smile, the touch of fingertips or a gush of tears with open and admitted artifice. In the midst of his most touching and pathetic creations, the artist is to be found, with his bag of tricks palpably open, his handkerchief ready, pointing out the emotional nuances, displaying his own reactions and feelings, inviting the reader to take part in a tripartite feast of sensations. Sterne the sentimentalist is actually Sterne the impressionist. His pathos is almost always couched in terms of personal reaction, and it is doubtful that even his saddest tableaux produced any real emotional shock among his readers. Had Sterne's purpose been high tragedy, then his work must be counted a failure, for even in its most pathetic implications it does not strike with the forceful impact of tragedy. Rather it sits gently upon the reader's heart, evoking a wistful nostalgia, a tender compassion. This, in fact, was Sterne's entire purpose—not to strike his readers with the sharp blows of tragedy, but to stir up for them the pleasurable, gentle bouquet of sadness. It was his purpose to "play upon the sentiments." Critics may argue the worthiness or sincerity of this as a literary creed, but the fact is that Sterne's work has survived through nearly two centuries; at its best it has produced portraits and tableaux that are unforgettable.

It is not easy to present a concise definition of "sentimentalism" as Sterne conceived it. The word has taken on a disreputable aura of bathos and a maudlin sexual overtone in our time. But in Sterne's age, on the Continent as well as in England, it was understood in the sense in which Sterne meant it. Within a short time after the appearance of *A Sentimental Journey*, a flood of imitations appeared, and some enterprising publisher even inaugurated a *Sentimental Magazine*. There was something about Sterne's sentimentalism that was peculiarly in tune with the tempo and attitude of the age. People who could weep gently at the artificial moral pieces that were seriously offered in the theater as high drama could equally be expected to drop a gentle tear or two into a scented handkerchief over passages of Sterne's most affecting sentimentalisms.

Today Sterne's artifices are clearly apparent. It is difficult to imagine anyone weeping over *A Sentimental Journey*. Our age is attuned to a deeper understanding of tragedy and a justified contempt for the obviously maudlin. Nevertheless, we can be appreciative of the delicate whimsy of Sterne's humor, and the gentle strokes of his emotional game. *A Sentimental Journey* is still a delight-

ful experience in reading, and remains the most popular
and best known of Sterne's books.

At Calais Sterne purchased a chaise from Monsieur Dessein, and began the trip to Paris. At Montreuil, where he
stayed at the Hotel de la Cour de France, he engaged a
valet on the recommendation of the innkeeper. This
man we know by the name Sterne gave him, La Fleur, as
wayward and gay as his master, always in love with some
chambermaid or peasant girl.

> .... he was a faithful, affectionate, simple soul as
> ever trudged after the heels of a philosopher; and
> notwithstanding his talents of drum-beating and
> splatterdash-making, which, though very good in
> themselves, happened to be of no great service to me,
> yet I was hourly recompensed by the festivity of his
> temper——it supplied all defects——I had a constant
> resource in his looks, in all difficulties and distresses
> of my own——I was going to have added, of his too;
> but La Fleur was out of the reach of every thing; for
> whether it was hunger or thirst, or cold or nakedness,
> or watchings, or whatever stripes of ill luck La Fleur
> met with in our journeyings, there was no index in
> his physiognomy to point them out by——he was eter-
> nally the same . . .

With La Fleur to look after his needs, Sterne continued
on to Paris. There was a large colony of fashionable English, resident in the city, and Sterne was welcomed into
their circle. Among them was John "Fish" Crawford,
who was to receive the first word of Sterne's death in London two years later; Sir James Macdonald, a young Scot,
who figures in the memoirs of many literary men of the
period, including Boswell; Lord Ossory, and many others
of Sterne's friends. The French, too, accepted Sterne
warmly, and he showed himself again a master of adaptation, outdoing the French in etiquette, jollity, and all the

other traits which stand high in the character of the people. But he tired more quickly than ever of the artificiality of this life. "For three weeks together," he recalled, "I was of every man's opinion I met.——*Pardi! ce Mons. Yorick a autant d'esprit que nous autres——Il raisonne bien,* said another——*C'est un bon enfant,* said a third.—— And at this price I could have eaten and drank and been merry all the days of my life at Paris; but 'twas a dishonest *reckoning*——I grew ashamed of it.——It was the gain of a slave——every sentiment of honour revolted against it—— the higher I got, the more was I forced upon my *beggarly system*——the better the *Coterie*——the more children of Art——I languish'd for those of Nature: and one night, after a most vile prostitution of myself to half a dozen different people, I grew sick——went to bed——order'd La Fleur to get me horses in the morning to set out for Italy."

In reading this, it must be kept in mind that Sterne wrote it under the influence of a wave of moral remorse—a by-product of his passion for Eliza Draper. He may have exaggerated the horror with which he looked upon his prostitution as a jester; this aspect of it had seldom troubled him before. Nevertheless, he remained only three weeks in Paris, setting out about the first of November for Italy, in company with several Englishmen, and taking with him the redoubtable La Fleur. From this point on, we have not even the misleading hints of *A Sentimental Journey,* for death cut short Sterne's fanciful account. But in the letters he addressed to his banker, Panchaud, in Paris, we can trace his journey into Italy.

At Lyons the party stopped several days, and had a "joyous time there,—dining and supping every day at the Commandant's." Several of the group of Englishmen remained in Lyons, and Sterne pushed on with the others. By November 7, they had gone as far as Pont Beauvoisin, where they found themselves marooned, the roads through the mountains being impassable because of floods resulting from melting snows. "For how long the gentlemen, who are my fellow-travellers, and myself, shall languish in this state of vexatious captivity, Heaven and Earth surely know; for it rains as if they were coming together to settle the matter." Within a few days, however, they were able to continue. But the passes through the Savoy mountains were treacherous, and eight days were required for the passage. By the eighteenth of the month Sterne arrived in Turin, his first Italian city. Again he was halted by rains, travel to Milan having been rendered impossible. But he enjoyed every minute of the two weeks he spent in the city. "—I am very happy, and have found my way into a dozen houses already.—To-morrow I am to be presented to the King; and when that ceremony is over, I shall have my hands full of engagements." Sterne found few Englishmen in Turin, but he was happy to find his friend Sir James Macdonald. About a fortnight after arriving in the city, he left in company with Macdonald for Milan.

At Milan occurred the meeting with the Marchesa Fagniani, who figures in *A Sentimental Journey.* This acquaintance, he averred, gave him "more pleasure than any one I had the honour to make in Italy." As usual, Sterne exaggerated the importance of the incident, for he could not have had more than a few flying glimpses of the lady in his brief stay in Milan. Then Sterne and Macdonald traveled onward, passing through Parma, Piacenza, and Bologna. By the eighteenth of December the two men were in Florence, where they remained three days, dining with Sir Horace Mann, recently appointed minister. But Sterne was looking forward to Rome—". . . in five days shall tread the Vatican, and be introduced to all the saints in the Pantheon." With the civilities over in Florence, they hurried on, and by Christmas time they were in Rome.

No record has come to light of Sterne's activities in Rome on this occasion. He planned to remain two weeks, and undoubtedly was well received, as in London and Paris. No doubt he trod the Vatican, and saw the religious landmarks of the ancient city. But it is highly doubtful that he had an audience with the Pope; although no feeling of delicacy would have kept Sterne from meeting the head of a church he had so bitterly attacked, yet it seems doubtful that he would have failed to mention it in his letters or writings, had such a meeting taken place.

If Sterne continued his "sentimental journey" as he planned, he left Rome early in the new year, and by about the middle of January, 1766, he was in Naples, where he had decided to spend the winter months. At Naples he fell in with a gay company of Englishmen and Italian leaders of fashion, and he thoroughly enjoyed himself. The climate, entertainment and gay companions seemed to agree with him, and by the time he had been a fortnight in the city, he assured Hall-Stevenson that he was growing "fat, sleek, and well liking; not improving in stature, but in breadth." He declared himself "happy as a king," and wrote enthusiastically of his life here:

> We have a jolly carnival of it; nothing but operas, punchinelloes, festinoes, and masquerades. We (that is *nous autres*) are all dressing out for one this night at the Princess Francavivalla's, which is to be superb. The English dine with her (exclusively): and so much for small chat,—except that I saw a little comedy last week, with more expression and spirit, and true character, than I shall see one hastily again.

To Lydia he wrote that he found himself "infinitely better than I was, and hope to have added at least ten years to my life, by this journey to Italy . . ." Alas! poor Yorick. Sterne grasped eagerly at straws, and the slightest improvement in his fragile health sent him into superlative declarations. The Italian journey fell far short of adding ten years to his life. The seeds of his bodily corruption had been sowed years before, and the threads of his life were snapping one by one.

The same air which seemed to Sterne to be giving him new vigor was playing havoc with his young friend, Sir James Macdonald. The young man, then only in his twenty-fifth year, was stricken immediately on his arrival in Naples. The two men planned to return to Rome before Easter, in company with a Mr. Errington, Sterne's friend of several years' standing. When the time came for the departure from Naples, Macdonald had not yet recovered, and he carried to Rome the illness from which he died in July of that year, two months after he had parted from Sterne. He was mourned as a young man of great promise, and it is something of a tribute to Sterne's character that he could have found high favor with a man of Macdonald's stamp.

Again details are lacking of Sterne's second visit to Rome. He probably remained in the city about a month, and left one lasting memento of his stay. This was a bust in terra-cotta by Nollekens, remarkable for its life and strength of features. If the bust can be taken as a good likeness, Sterne had indeed brought new vigor out of Naples. The eyes are expressive, without the sharp, satyr-like quality of the first Reynolds portrait. The nose is strong, the mouth is firm, with full lips, and the chin had lost much of the sharpness of the earlier likeness. In this bust there is little of the wild Parson Yorick which Reynolds caught so admirably; but perhaps there is a foresight of the sentimental Sterne of his last two years.

There are many traditions regarding this month in Rome. It was said that he was pinched for money, and often wandered the streets, an object of pity. This tradition has been so long laid that it is only mentioned here as an example of the wild stories which grew up around the man. The fact is that he had used very little of the credit he had arranged for, and his letters to Panchaud and Foley show him the master of his finances that winter.

Sterne had expected to complete the tour as companion to a gentleman, possibly Errington. The itinerary, as he gave it to Hall-Stevenson, was to include Vienna, Saxony, Berlin, "and so by the Spa, and thence through Holland to England." However, before leaving Rome, he changed his mind, and decided to return to England more directly. Perhaps differences had arisen over the matter of the route, for Sterne wished to see his wife and daughter before going back to Yorkshire.

The concern manifested by Sterne over the well-being of his wife and daughter should be enough to give him a character in the eyes of the strictest moralist. Throughout his travels, his thoughts went constantly back to them, and at regular intervals his letters went out, under enclosure to his banker, to be transmitted to them. He was conscientious in the matter of money, and he assured Foley that any uneasiness on Mrs. Sterne's part, on that account, "is doubly so to me." Hearing from Lydia that the climate of Tours had made them both ill, he advised them to "fly" from there at once. As early as February, he was making plans to be reunited with them in the spring, and hoped to take them with him back to England:

> I desire you will get your mother to write to Mr. C.,
> that I may discharge every debt; and then, my Lydia,
> if I live, the produce of my pen shall be yours: if Fate
> reserves me not that, the humane and good (part for

thy father's sake, part for thy own) will never aban-
don thee!—If your mother's health will permit her to
return with me to England, your summers I will ren-
der as agreeable as I can at Coxwould; your winters
at York.

With this intention, Sterne left Rome about the first of
May. But before he arrived in France, Mrs. Sterne and
Lydia had moved several times, and Sterne followed after
them, receiving word of them as he went from town to
town. "Never man has been such a wildgoose chase after
a wife as I have been," he told Hall-Stevenson. "After
having sought her in five or six different towns, I found
her at last in *Franche Compté.*" He was delighted with
Lydia, finding her just as he would have wished. But the
interview with Mrs. Sterne—"poor woman!" Sterne wrote,
"she was very cordial, &c."—turned out not as he had
hoped. She insisted on remaining in France, and Sterne
again agreed, making provision with Panchaud for the
generous sum of three hundred pounds a year, although
he assured his banker that she was to be "confined to no
particular sum."

Anxious now to be back in England, Sterne parted once
more from Lydia and Mrs. Sterne. But there were still
a few gay evenings left to him before the Continental adventure drew to a close. At Dijon, he stopped at the château
of a friend, where he remained a week, "patriarching it"
with his hostess and "half a dozen of very handsome and
agreeable ladies." From the château he wrote Hall-Stevenson, "I am most unaccountably well, and most unaccountably nonsensical;—'tis at least a proof of good spirits;
which is a sign and token given me in these latter days,
that I must take up again the pen. In faith, I think I shall
die with it in my hand; but I shall live these ten years, My
Anthony—"

Promising to be with his "cousin Anthony" on the king's birthday, Sterne left Dijon for Paris. Here, according to his plans, he remained three days, long enough to dine with his friends and conclude his business on the Continent. Then, bidding farewell to France for the last time, he boarded the boat at Calais, and ended his "sentimental journey."

XVII

The Jester's Love

IF STERNE fulfilled his promise, he met Hall-Stevenson in London, and dined with him on the king's birthday. But he did not linger long in the city; he hurried on to York, and after several days there, he returned to his parsonage in Coxwould.

By the middle of July, he was again at work on *Shandy*. But he had altered his plans for this installment. Instead of writing two volumes, he proposed to write only one, in continuation of my uncle Toby's love affair with the Widow Wadman. Then he intended to write the story of his "agreeable tour" through France and Italy, in four volumes—two yearly installments of two volumes each. This would occupy him until 1769, when he planned again to undertake a continuation of *Tristram*. It was a well-laid plan, which miscarried only through the intervention of death.

This lonely summer at Coxwould was largely a repetition of the last. Although he described his parsonage as "my peaceful retreat," and philosophized prettily on the happiness which each man carries within himself, still he was far from happy. Sterne in solitude was seldom in his highest spirits, and this summer there were numerous burdens to bedevil him. His health, seemingly improved in Italy, was again bad, and his hemorrhages reappeared

with alarming frequency. His wife's extravagance proved
a constant drain on his resources, and several times that
summer he wrote to his bankers for further allowances to
his wife. His parish business, too, he found wearisome,
and in the solitude of his retreat his thoughts went often
back to Paris. Before autumn he was considering "a
jaunt" for six weeks, about Christmas time.

From Lydia came alarming news of Mrs. Sterne's failing
health. At one time Sterne was planning to go to Avignon
to be with her, if she continued to grow worse. However,
she recovered and began (albeit expensively) to mend.

The most interesting event of the summer, and one
which casts light on a humane side of Sterne's philosophy,
was an exchange of letters between him and one Ignatius
Sancho. This Sancho was a Negro, who had risen from
slavery and by dint of intensive application had educated
himself, and later wrote in imitation of Sterne. In July
Sterne received a letter from Sancho, who had been impressed by an incidental attack on slavery in one of Sterne's
sermons. "Of all my favorite authors, not one has drawn
a tear in favor of my miserable black brethren," Sancho
wrote, "—excepting yourself, and the humane author of
Sir Geo. Ellison." He hoped Sterne might further show
his humanity by inserting a plea for the oppressed slaves
in the next installment of *Shandy*.

> —I think you will forgive me,—I am sure you will
> applaud me,—for beseeching you to give one half-
> hour's attention to slavery, as it is this day practiced
> in our West Indies. That subject handled in your
> striking manner, would ease the yoke (perhaps of
> many;) but if only of one,—gracious God! what a feast
> to a benevolent heart. . . . Dear Sir, think in me you
> behold the uplifted hands of thousands of my brother
> Moors. Grief (you pathetically observe) is eloquent:
> figure to yourself their attitudes, hear their supplicat-

ing addresses!—alas! you cannot refuse. Humanity
must comply—

The letter suited exactly the mood of philosophical
melancholy in which it found Sterne. He sat down and
wrote a long reply, admirable for its expression of a prob-
lem which had undoubtedly troubled Sterne often. He
remarked the strange coincidences of fate: the letter had
caught him at work on the touching story of a Negro girl
in bondage, which he expected to work into the next installment of his book (and did—in the corporal's account
of his brother Tom). Sterne expressed, in his answer, a
philosophy that found its way into the pages of his books:

> It is by the finest tints and most insensible gradations
> that Nature descends from the fairest face about St.
> James's to the sootiest complexion in Africa.—At
> which tint of these is it, that the ties of blood are to
> cease? and how many shades must we descend lower
> still in the scale, ere mercy is to vanish with them?
> But 'tis no uncommon thing, my good Sancho, for
> one half of the world to use the other half of it like
> brutes, and then endeavour to make them so. For
> my own part, I never look *westward* (when I am in a
> pensive mood at least) but I think of the burdens
> which our brothers and sisters are *there* carrying. . . .
> for, in serious truth, it casts a sad shade upon the
> world, that so great a part of it are, and have been so
> long, bound in chains of darkness, and in chains of
> misery. . . .

Sterne fulfilled his promise to Sancho, and included in
the ninth volume a plea for the oppressed. He made his
plea doubly effective by its wit. He had the good sense
to understand that a sentimental harangue might have
done this cause a disservice:

> A negro has a soul? an' please your honour, said the
> corporal (doubtingly).

I am not much versed, corporal, quoth my uncle Toby, in things of that kind; but I suppose God would not leave him without one, any more than thee or me—

——It would be putting one sadly over the head of another, quoth the corporal.

It would so; said my uncle Toby. Why, then, an' please your honour, is a black wench to be used worse than a white one?

I can give no reason, said my uncle Toby——

—Only, cried the corporal, shaking his head, because she has no one to stand up for her—

—'Tis that very thing, Trim, quoth my uncle Toby, —which recommends her to protection—and her brethren with her; 'tis the fortune of war which has put the whip into our hands now——where it may be hereafter, heaven knows!—but be it where it will, the brave, Trim! will not use it unkindly.

Hardly a revolutionary philosophy today, when the intelligent part of the world adopts this view as a truism. But Sterne wrote nearly two hundred years ago, when England was just setting out on her career of world imperialism, and black slavery was accepted by the entire English-speaking world. Yet, even today, it is an heretical philosophy in many parts of the world.

By late autumn Sterne's spirits had again improved. The York races that year saw a gala event in town—the attendance of the Duke of York. In his honor there was a play at the theatre and a ball in the Assembly Rooms. Sterne, whose friendship with the Duke has already been noted, came down to York for the festivities, and preached a sermon on Sunday, as a fitting conclusion to a week of gaiety. All the dignitaries of the cathedral and the city were present to hear Sterne preach, and Parson Yorick shared the spotlight with the Duke. The gay activities over, Sterne returned to his unfinished volume of *Shandy*, and in several weeks completed it.

The news from abroad was also heartening to Sterne. His wife's illness had apparently passed, and she had taken a house for the winter. Lydia wrote that her French was improving, and she had attracted a wealthy young Marquis as a suitor. By late autumn Sterne had been able, also, to clear his credit by balancing his wife's account.

Late in November he was again ready for his annual London campaign. To Panchaud he wrote gaily, "I am going to lie-in of another child of the Shandaic procreation, in town.—I hope you wish me a safe delivery." However, he was delayed in starting, and it was not until early in January, 1767, that he brought his brain-child into the city. He took lodgings over a wig-maker's shop at number 41 Old Bond Street, just off Piccadilly—a most fashionable address—and embarked on his usual round of activities. Garrick was on view in a new play at the Drury Lane, and Sterne went often to the theatre. He dined with Lord Ossory, and was again taken up by the Duke of York. Before his visit was a week old, it began to appear that this season would be his most brilliant in London.

The weather was a constant topic of conversation in the city through the month of January. The first week of the new year it began to snow, and the snow continued at intervals until the middle of the month. The cold was so intense that Sterne could "scarse lay in bed for it." His health was affected by the cold and he suffered cruelly. By the sixteenth there was "a dead stagnation of everything, and scarse any talk but about the damages done over the Kingdom by this cruel storm." Reports came in that the York stagecoach had missed a bridge in the storm and had plunged into the river with fourteen passengers; by evening the report was contradicted, and the city

laughed at its own nervousness. Thawing weather brought
with it streets slushy with mud and water. Sterne assured
a friend that "the streets are dirtier than in the town of
Coxwould—for they are up to the knees, except on the
trottoire."

By the end of the month the ninth volume of *Tristram
Shandy* was ready for its readers. The response was most
gratifying, and Sterne was able to report happily that it
was received better than any of its predecessors. Sterne
apologized for having written only one volume, explain-
ing that illness had kept him from continuing. However,
this must have been a subterfuge, for he had planned to
write only a single volume for this installment. This volume certainly deserved the warm welcome it received,
for it is among Sterne's best. His description of my uncle
Toby's attack on the citadel of the Widow Wadman's
heart, in the manner of a militarist, is a keen bit of non-
sense, as well as satire. Sterne skirted here the very edge
of decency, but his suggestiveness was so well flavored with
wit that it could hardly offend any intelligent reader.
Aside from the main thread of the volume—my uncle
Toby's campaign of love—there are many other fine passages, which rank with Sterne's best. His pretty plea for
the oppressed has already been noted; the story of Maria,
the heartbroken peasant girl, found wide favor; and Sterne
showed the delicate touch of which his pen was capable in
the passage on time, dedicated to his "dear Jenny."

> Time wastes too fast: every letter I trace tells me with
> what rapidity Life follows my pen; the days and hours
> of it, more precious, my dear Jenny! than the rubies
> about thy neck, are flying over our heads like the
> light clouds of a windy day, never to return more—
> every thing presses on—whilst thou art twisting that
> lock,—see! it grows grey; and every time I kiss thy

hand to bid adieu, and every absence which follows it, are preludes to that eternal separation which we are shortly to make.—

But even now, Sterne's critics were not prepared to concede him anything. Hardly had the book come off the press when they again opened the attack. Their volleys were aimed, as usual, at the indecencies of his work. These criticisms were followed by open letters to the newspapers. Sterne met these attacks with his usual scorn, and at least one section of his critics sought recourse to his church superiors. An anonymous letter was sent to Robert Hays Drummond, then Archbishop of York. "Several well wishers to your Grace, and to religion and the cause of virtue, modesty, and decency, think it a duty incumbent on them, consistently with that regard they have for them, as well as order and right conduct, to refer your Grace to a letter, signed *Davus*, in the *Public Ledger* of this day, very justly, as they humbly think, animadverting on the scandal they have long taken and oftener conceived at the works of 'Tristram Shandy,' as written by a *clergyman* and a *dignified* one, uncensured by his superiors." The letter urged the Archbishop to use whatever means his discretion might dictate, to "deter this wanton scandal to his cloth, from proceeding in this lewd, ludicrous manner, as he has long done, to the shame and disgrace of his sacred order and the detriment of society." It closed with a plea for the daughters who had been corrupted by Sterne's lewdness.

The letter is typical of this particular section of Sterne's critics, and something of this view has found its way into almost everything ever written about him, even by the most rational of critics. Yet the possibility of corrupting influence could be charged equally to Shakespeare, whose language must often be as harsh to delicate ears as Sterne's. It could be charged equally to Chaucer, who stands account-

able for more than one suggestive passage. A moral—if
there is one—must be drawn from the obvious fact that an
intelligent, healthy mind gives all things their just due.
Such a mind is not corrupted by a suggestive word or epi-
sode, but finds enjoyment in wit. As for other minds—intelligent critics have long given up their rescue from the
degradations of literature. It is accepted as a truism that
the most easily inflammable mind is the quickest to find
offense in books and plays. Much of the Victorian attitude
we now trace to this underlying psychological phenom-
enon. It is sad but true that the Victorian critique persists
tenaciously where Sterne is concerned, long after it has
found itself outmoded elsewhere.

Apparently Archbishop Drummond was not too deeply
impressed with the dangers lurking in Sterne's lewdness.
He adopted the intelligent view that a work of genius
more than balances the possible risk to corruptible daughters, and if he ever mentioned the letter to Sterne, it was
merely by way of information, not censure. Sterne was
warmly welcomed at Bishopthorpe, and even made the
Archbishop his confidant in an affair of the heart.

This affair of the heart, Sterne's love for Eliza Draper,
is the final enigma of Sterne's amazing character. The
contradictions and paradoxes with which the last year of
Sterne's life was crowded have made it doubly difficult
to find the man behind the maze. Was his love for Eliza
real or feigned? And what of his denials to Lydia and
Mrs. Sterne? And his concern for them? Are they, too,
genuine? The too revealing story of Sterne's love for
Eliza is found in his *Journal to the Bramine*. But it can
be interpreted only when read side by side with his letters
of this period. The truth is here, behind the paradoxes,
but only for those who can weigh each clue in the enigma.

Soon after Sterne's arrival in London for this season, he met Commodore William James, who had gained fame and honor as a naval officer. It had been his duty to protect England's East Indian venture by ridding the sea of pirates who lay in wait for the merchant vessels. James had carried the news of war with the French to Clive in India, and in many other services had made himself a hero. In 1759 he returned to England and the honors that awaited him. He was made chairman of the board of directors of the East India Company, and later he was raised to the peerage. To the house of the Jameses in Soho Sterne often came, and a strong intimacy grew up between the errant Yorick and Mr. and Mrs. James. Because of Commodore James' position in Anglo-Indian matters, his house was a gathering point for visiting Indian notables, and among these was Eliza Draper.

Eliza was only twenty-three when Sterne met her, early in January, 1767. Her father, May Sclater, head of the East Indian settlement at Anjengo, died when Eliza was a tiny child. Under the guardianship of her grandfather, she was educated in England, but returned to India, where she was married, at the age of fourteen, to Daniel Draper. Draper, twenty years older than his child-wife, was a stolid, humorless Englishman, who was rising swiftly in the East India Company. The marriage, while it could hardly have been one of love, was nevertheless considered a good match. Two children were born, a boy and a girl, and in 1765 the Drapers came to England to arrange for the education of the children. Draper, after spending some time in England, returned to India, leaving Eliza among her relatives in the mother country. Her health had been endangered by the climate of India and the birth of her two children, and an immediate return seemed inadvisable.

Eliza, despite a plainness of person, had a charm which

attracted many admirers. Thrust into the center of London's polite society just as she was emerging from girlhood, she found it pleasant to engage in the little flirtations of the fashionable. Little by little her unattractive, stolid husband disappeared into the background; her marriage, which she had long ago realized was a mistake, now appeared as a burden, and she dreaded the time when she might have to return to India.

Often a guest at the James house, Eliza was thrilled one night to find among her fellow guests Mr. Sterne, who was being honored by all London. Sterne found the young woman, at their first meeting, quite ordinary in appearance. "I beheld you," he later confessed, "as an object of compassion, and as a very plain woman. The mode of your dress (though fashionable) disfigured you." But Yorick saw—or thought he saw—in her something more than a plain woman. "I never saw so intelligent, so animated, so good a countenance. . . . A something in your eyes and voice, you possess in a degree more persuasive than any woman I ever saw, read, or heard of."

Eliza, flattered at Sterne's attentions, encouraged him, and Sterne, who had gaily described to his friend Woodhouse the formula for sentimental love-making, soon found himself the victim of the game. His poor, foolish, unstable heart was lost to this girl who was hardly older than his daughter Lydia. This love was a passion that strangely enslaved Sterne in the remaining months of his life. The similar flirtations with Lady Percy, Mrs. Vesey, and the rest faded from his thoughts, and even the memory of Kitty de Fourmantelle—vividly with him as he wrote the passage on time to his "dear Jenny" last summer—was driven from his mind and heart by this new love.

As always in the affairs of the heart, Sterne rapidly dispensed with formalities. His intimacy with Eliza ripened quickly, and within a few weeks after their first meeting he sent her his books, with this frank note:

> Eliza will receive my books with this. The sermons came all hot from the heart. I wish that I could give them any title to be offered to yours. The others came from the head: I am more indifferent about their reception.
>
> I know not how it comes about, but I am half in love with you; I ought to be wholly so; for I never valued (or saw more good qualities to value) or thought more of one of your sex than of you; so adieu.

Eliza was pleased at this frank avowal. Sterne called on her, and a delightful fancy grew up between them: she called her admirer Bramin, the giver of all knowledge, and Sterne retaliated by naming her his Bramine.

Characteristically, Sterne made no effort to conceal his affair from the world. What has often been described as a want of discretion in him was rather an amazing frankness. He saw nothing wrong in his flirtations, and he confided his loves to the world. Mr. and Mrs. James were soon made aware of the love between Bramin and Bramine, and Sterne made Eliza the subject of his conversation wherever he went. He dined with Lord Bathurst, the old patron who had known Addison, Pope, and Swift—"but thou, Eliza, wert the star that conducted and enliven'd the discourse. . . . I was heard (as I talked of thee an hour without intermission) with so much pleasure and attention, that the good old Lord toasted your health three different times." They appeared together publicly, and the attachment became a matter of gossip in London society.

It was not long before news of the affair traveled—as such news will—across the channel to Mrs. Sterne, who was recuperating at Avignon. Not more than four weeks after

Sterne's first meeting with Eliza, some traveling crone was able to bring Mrs. Sterne the juicy tidbit of gossip which emanated from Piccadilly, regarding her husband's East Indian darling. Rumors of a separation between the Sternes had been prevalent before, and Mrs. Sterne was made "uneasy" by this new report. In her letter to her father, Lydia wrote at length of her mother's distress. When the story was brought to her, Mrs. Sterne told her informer that she did not wish to hear it, and forbade further discussion of it. Nevertheless, Lydia sought denial from her father, and Sterne gave it. "—I do not wish to know who was the busy fool who made your mother uneasy," he wrote of Eliza. " 'Tis true I have a friendship for her, but not to infatuation.—I believe I have judgment enough to discern hers, and every woman's faults."

That was late in February, and if Sterne still retained any judgment then, he was soon parted from it. Through March his letters to Eliza spoke of his growing passion. The face that he had at first found plain, and her eyes, he now declared were "perfections that must strike the most indifferent judge, because they are equal to any of God's works in a similar way, and finer than any I beheld in all my travels . . ." He threw judgment to the winds, and his heart after it: He proposed marriage to her—in the improbable event that the death of Draper and Mrs. Sterne should leave them both free. " 'Tis true, I am ninety-five in constitution, and you but twenty-five;——rather too great a disparity this!—but what I want in youth, I will make up in wit and good humor.—Not Swift so loved his Stella, Scarron his Maintenon, or Waller his Sacharissa, as I will love and sing thee, my wife elect! All those names, eminent as they were, shall give place to thine, Eliza."

The drama of Sterne's love moved on rapidly to its climax. The villain of the piece had already struck, and

about the first of March Eliza received a letter from her
husband asking her to return home at once. Draper, not
unwise in the ways of the world, may have had forebodings
of what was now taking place in London.

The letter came as a shock to Eliza, and in grief she took
to her bed. Sterne, calling that very day, found her con-
fined to her room, and was told by the servant that Mrs.
Draper could receive no one. Returning to Old Bond
Street, Sterne wrote an anxious letter and sent it over to
Eliza by messenger the next morning:

> I cannot rest, Eliza, though I shall call on you at
> half past twelve, till I know how you do.—May thy
> dear face smile, as thou risest like the sun of this
> morning. I was much grieved to hear of your alarm-
> ing indisposition yesterday; and disappointed, too, at
> not being let in.—Remember, my dear, that a friend
> has the same right as a physician. The etiquettes of
> this town (you'll say) say otherwise.—No matter.
> Delicacy and propriety do not always consist in ob-
> serving their rigid doctrines.
> I am going out to breakfast, but shall be at my
> lodgings by eleven: when I hope to read a single line
> under thy own hand, that thou art better, and wilt
> be glad to see thy Bramin.

Eliza, it turned out, would indeed be glad to see her
Bramin. Sterne called that day, and often in the weeks
that followed. Together they lamented the fate that had
brought them face to face for a brief moment and now was
tearing them from each other's company.

As the time drew nearer for Eliza's departure, Sterne
protested more volubly his love. He wanted her to delay
her departure for another year. "I am firmly persuaded
within my own heart," he wrote, "that thy husband could
never limit thee with regard to time." He urged Eliza
to write to Draper, and plead with him the cause of her

health. However, Draper had protested already against the heavy expense of Eliza's long stay in London, and the dutiful wife prepared sadly for the long voyage to India.

The East Indian vessel *Earl of Chatham* was at Deal awaiting favorable winds for the sailing. Eliza made arrangements for passage, said her last tearful good-byes in London, and went to Deal to await the ship's departure. During the short time she remained in Deal, Sterne wrote to her daily, and made every arrangement for her comfort at sea. He instructed her regarding the tuning of the pianoforte he had given her for her cabin. He sent a hammer and pliers for this purpose; in the same parcel he sent down ten brass screws to hang her clothing on—"I purchased twelve; but stole a couple from you to put up in my own cabin, at Coxwould," he explained. "I shall never hang, nor take my hat off one of them, but I shall think of you." To the pilot at Deal, Sterne sent instructions to purchase a comfortable armchair for his departing love.

News came from Deal. The ship was still in port, delayed by unfavorable winds. Sterne visited his friends, the Jameses, and all wept for their unhappy young friend. They made plans to go together to Deal for a last visit with Eliza, if the sailing should again be delayed. In the meantime Sterne could only cherish her portrait. "But what is that," he wrote unhappily, "to the original?" He was concerned at the ill-effect of fresh paint in her cabin upon her health. "The fresh painting will be enough to destroy every nerve about thee. Nothing so pernicious as white lead. Take care of yourself, dear girl; and sleep not in it too soon: it will be enough to give you a stroke of an epilepsy."

The winds decreed that Sterne was not to see his Bramine again. With a favorable breeze, the ship prepared for

departure, and on April 3, 1767, the *Earl of Chatham*
raised its sails for the long and dangerous voyage. A long
farewell letter reached Eliza just before the ship sailed.
The London papers had reported fair winds and the im-
pending departure, and Sterne hastened to write a last
billet:

> —blessed woman! take my last, last farewell!—Cher-
> ish the remembrance of me; think how I esteem, nay
> how affectionately I love thee, and what a price I set
> upon thee! Adieu, adieu! and with my adieu—let me
> give thee one streight rule of conduct, that thou hast
> heard from my lips in a thousand forms—but I con-
> center it in one word,
>   Reverence Thyself.
>   Adieu, once more, Eliza! May no anguish of heart
> plant a wrinkle upon thy face, till I behold it again!

Before the Bramin had parted from his Bramine, they
had exchanged gifts. Eliza's gift to Sterne had been some
handkerchiefs from India, and Sterne wrote that they had
received a baptism of his blood, from another hemorrhage
of the lungs. "My bleeding is quite stopped, and I feel
the principle of life strong within me," he assured her, "so
be not alarmed, Eliza—" Before they parted, they had also
exchanged journals, in which each had written intimate
thoughts of their weeks together. They agreed to continue
this journal in the months during which they would be
parted, and to exchange these diaries again when they
were reunited.

The journal which Sterne kept in the following months
came to light in the middle of the last century, and has
been published as the *Journal to Eliza* or the *Journal to
the Bramine*. It affords an intimate glimpse of Sterne's
inner existence in the last months of his life, yet it is misleading, unless read side by side with the other letters and

papers of this period. Ostensibly the journal shows a man torn by grief over his departing love. Sterne protested his passion and his anguish over their separation . . . "—dark to me is all this world without thee! and most heavily will pass every hour over my head, till that is come which brings thee, dear Woman back to Albion," he wrote in his first entry, on April 13. Her departure left him "worn out with fevers of all kinds, but most, by that fever of the heart with which I'm eternally wasting, and shall waste till I see Eliza again." He read her letters over a hundred times, sitting with her picture before him and crying out, "O my Bramine! my Friend! my Help-mate!" He consoled himself with the thought that, sad as the parting was, some day they would be happily reunited. He visited the Jameses in Gerrard Street, and had long conversations about Eliza. His heart sank at an "infamous account of Draper and his detested Character at Bombay." "For what a wretch art thou hazarding thy life, my dear friend," he cried, "and what thanks is his nature capable of returning? —thou wilt be repaid with injuries and insults!"

Buying a chart of the ocean, he followed the progress of her ship, as he estimated it from day to day. "Oh! tis but a little way off—and I could venture after it in a boat, methinks—" After a Sunday night dinner at the Jameses, he talked of Eliza and "burst into tears a dozen different times." The next day he was ill and confined to his rooms. He called in a surgeon to bleed him, and after losing twelve ounces of blood he was weakened, rather than improved. "Alas! alas! the only Physician, and who carries the Balm of my Life along with her,—is Eliza."

Sterne's illness, whether caused by a broken heart or a weakened lung, was indeed serious. About three weeks after Eliza sailed, Sterne was lying on the verge of death. The fortitude which had seen him through these crises before served him now, and he began to improve. This most recent crisis had been aggravated by Sterne's use of James' powder, a dangerous medical nostrum. The physician Sterne called in diagnosed the illness as a venereal case, and there ensued an argument in a Shandaic vein:

> ——'tis impossible at least to be that, replied I—for I have had no commerce whatever with the sex—not even with my wife, added I, these 15 years—You are * * * * * however my good friend, said the Surgeon, or there is no such case in the world—what the Devil! said I without knowing woman—we will not reason about it, said the Physician—

In anger, Sterne dismissed the doctors, but as his suffering increased, he called them back to treat him. During his illness, Sterne's rooms had seen a steady procession of London's great. In one day he was visited by forty friends. As his strength returned, he began to make plans for his departure for Coxwould. He estimated that his illness would delay his departure by three weeks, and he hoped to start back home about the middle of May. In the last few days of April he suffered a relapse, but on the first day of May he was able to be out. Walking in the park, he met an earlier love (could it have been the beautiful Lady Percy?), but he no longer had eyes or thoughts for anyone but his Bramine.

The next day he suffered another relapse, and called again for his physician. As Molly, the servant-girl, came in to serve tea, she spoke of the days when she had laid a place for Mrs. Draper at this very table. Sterne wept bitter tears for his lost Bramine!

A few days later he was again up and about, going to a concert—one of the entertainments given at Carlisle House by Mrs. Theresa Cornelys, to which all fashionable London was flocking that season. His friends, who had been inquiring after him, prepared a round of dinners for him, and even when he was ready to leave London, he was detained by Lord and Lady Spencer, who had made plans to entertain him at dinner. He talked of Eliza, and found Lady Spencer very sympathetic.

On Friday, May 22, Sterne left London. He was so weak that he was forced to spend the week end at Newark, and before he continued his journey Monday morning, he scribbled a note to Hall-Stevenson:

> My dear Cousin——I have got conveyed thus far like a bale of cadaverous goods consigned to Pluto and company——lying in the bottom of my chaise most of the route, upon a large pillow which I had the *prevoyance* to purchase before I set out——I am worn out. . . . I know not what is the matter with me—but some *derangement* presses hard upon this machine——

At York, Sterne stopped for a visit with Archbishop Drummond, and at the prelate's urging he remained at Bishopthorpe for two days. Here, as everywhere, Sterne insisted on talking of Eliza. He showed the portrait of the Bramine to his Grace and to the Archbishop's wife and sister. They proved an interested group, and Sterne found them sympathetic in his distress. By Thursday Sterne felt strong enough to make the last stage of his trip, from York to Coxwould, and he arrived in his peaceful retreat a week after leaving London.

His first days in the parsonage Sterne spent in his bed, too weak to arise. He underwent a treatment of corrosive mercury, but the medicines were playing havoc with him, and he gave them all up, finding in the clear air and pleasant surroundings of Coxwould an effective tonic. He mended more rapidly here than in town, and ten days after his arrival found him again "as happy as a prince." "I wish," he wrote to his friend Lee, "you could see in how princely a manner I live; 'tis a land of plenty. I sit down alone to venison, fish, and wild fowl, or a couple of fowls or ducks, with curds, and strawberries, and cream, and all the simple plenty which a rich valley (under Hamilton Hills) can produce; with a clean cloth on my table, and a bottle of wine on my right hand to drink your health." He rode out every day with his two long-tailed horses drawing his chaise. He was much in the company of Hall-Stevenson, and the two men delighted in driving their chaises along the beach, running one wheel in the water, the other on the sand. Cousin Anthony visited Sterne at Coxwould, and the two men spent a day with Archbishop Drummond at York. With Hall-Stevenson, Sterne went to Harrogate for the waters and attended the York races in August.

On Sterne's arrival in York for the races, he received his first letter from Eliza. She had sent him the journal of her voyage, and Sterne read and re-read it, his emotions cut to shreds by the mere sight of her handwriting. All that summer he was envisioning a future—so he wrote in the journal—when they would be together. When he wandered out in the hills around Coxwould, he imagined Eliza at his side. Redecorating an apartment in the parsonage, he tried to arrange it as she would like it. "We shall be happy at last I know," he promised his Bramine, "—'tis the cornerstone of all my castles—and 'tis all I bargain for." At Skelton, at Harrogate, at Bishopthorpe, all of Yorick's conversation was of his Eliza, who combined in her all the virtues and beauties of womanhood. His friends were forced to listen to long eulogies of her, and it is testimony either to their patience or Sterne's powers of description that they never rebelled.

Yet, in spite of this show of passion, there are many indications that Sterne's love for Eliza Draper was less than the great love he painted it. His passionate protestations were sincere enough, for it was characteristic of the man that he could persuade himself into an obsession. Yet his passion was largely a passion of the mind; he delighted more in the game of love than in love itself. He toyed with passion, played with it in his mind, tortured himself with the miseries he could induce within himself. But his love for Eliza was not a blinding passion, of the sort that can lead men to acts of desperation. In short, Sterne accepted as his ideal of love the *grande passion;* he talked of it, he wrote of it, he played with the idea—but temperamentally he was incapable of such a love.

In the *Journal to the Bramine* Sterne was eloquent in his emotional confessions. He wrote eagerly of the day when he would be reunited with his love. However, we must read this along with his letters and actions of the period. Despite his protestations, he made no practical move to bring about the reunion. Had his love been strong enough, he could have kept Eliza in England. She dreaded the return to India; a word from Sterne, and Eliza would have remained in England, to face, if necessary, the scandal of divorce. Yet this word Sterne was unwilling to give; in fact, as far as we can determine from the journal and letters, it never seems to have occurred to him that as a lover he could seek a practical fruition of his love. He was happy in his misery, and he wrote passionately of his disordered emotions. The real depth of Sterne's passion can be gauged by the fact that it never occurred to him to face the hazards of the divorce court for his love, and when Mrs. Sterne demanded a denial of the circulated gossip, Yorick obliged her glibly. As for the *Journal to the Bramine,* sincere though it was, it was undoubtedly written with an eye to posthumous publication. This must be kept in mind when reading it.

There has been fostered recently a strange attitude among readers and writers of biography: it has become almost tantamount to defamation, to admit that a man was incapable of *grande passion*. Let him be a great actor, a great author, a great statesman, or a great engineer—it matters little, unless he was also a great lover. Yet it is not particularly to Sterne's discredit that his great love was mostly a love of the mind. His genius suffers nothing by this truth, nor does his stature as a man become greater or smaller.

The difference between the affair with Eliza and half a dozen other of Sterne's flirtations is almost entirely in the circumstances. His love for her seems not to have exceeded his love for Kitty de Fourmantelle, or Lady Percy, or Mrs. Vesey. But Eliza, with a hated husband five thousand miles away, was a susceptible and eager subject. What started as a charming little flirtation developed, largely through auto-suggestion, into the form of a great love. Even while Sterne was writing of his longing for the Bramine in his journal, he knew that his love would never reach a practical determination—nor was a practical determination necessary to his game of passion—or desirable.

Sterne was not the only man whose pen was moved to eloquence by the beautiful eyes and shapely face of Eliza. Several years later Eliza's favor was eagerly sought by the politician Wilkes and William Combes, the author of *Dr. Syntax*. The Abbé Raynal went further in his passion than Sterne, and proposed an elopement to France. Ordinarily a sober and intelligent man, he allowed his passion to color his judgment, and penned a strange, half-mad passage in his *History of the Indies*:

> Territory of Anjengo, thou art nothing; but thou hast given birth to Eliza. A day will come when

these staples of commerce, founded by the Europeans on the coast of Asia, will exist no more. . . . But if my works are destined to have any duration, the name of Anjengo will not be obliterated from the memory of man. . . . There it is that Eliza Draper was born. . . . Eliza ended her days in the land of her forefathers, at the age of three-and-thirty. A celestial soul was separated from a heavenly body. . . . And thou, original writer, her admirer and her friend, it was Eliza who inspired thy works, and dictated to thee the most affecting pages of them. Fortunate Sterne, thou art no more, and I am left behind. I weep over thee with Eliza. . . .

Sterne never saw Eliza after those few short weeks in London. When she returned to England, it was as an eloper escaping from an irate husband. Sterne had been dead several years, and Eliza was in a bitter mood. "I believed Sterne, implicitly I believed him; I had no motive to do otherwise than believe him just, generous, and unhappy—till his death gave me to know that he was tainted with the vices of injustice, meanness, and folly," she wrote.

But all this was later, when Yorick's unhappy, stormy life had ended. In the summer of 1767 all this was far ahead. Sterne spent the summer in a dream of love, half real, completely fantastic. He scribbled his frank confessions in a journal for the world to read a century later.

This was the jester's love.

XVIII

The London Finale

FROM his summer dream of a perfect love Sterne had a harsh awakening. From France came news that Mrs. Sterne was preparing for a journey homeward. Although she was contented in France, the stories of her husband's indiscretions which floated over to her at intervals had disturbed her, and had made her especially uneasy regarding her financial position. She was dependent entirely on Sterne for her existence, having surrendered her independent income. Sterne never forgot the responsibility which thus rested on him, and throughout he appears to have dealt most honorably with his wife, financially at least. But Mrs. Sterne was unwilling to risk her comfort on her husband's whims any longer, and she was coming to England for a financial settlement.

In his letters to France during the spring and summer Sterne revealed himself paradoxically. While he was complaining in his journal and to his friends of the grief in his heart at the loss of Eliza, he was writing to Lydia:

—I am unhappy,—thy mother and thyself at a distance from me; and what can compensate for such destitution?—For God's sake, persuade her to come and fix in England, for life is too short to waste in separation; and, whilst she lives in one country, and

I in another, many people will suppose it proceeds from choice;—besides, I want thee near me, thou child and darling of my heart!—I am in a melancholy mood. . . .

And in the very next line, he was describing the charms of his Eliza—a "drooping lily," this "incomparable woman." It is difficult to read logic into such a letter, unless we remember that Sterne the realist and man of the world is far different from Sterne the sentimentalist and dreamer. Eliza was the fit subject of a sentimental dream, but his love for her never struck him as a matter for practical considerations. Sterne expected the world to regard his love as a pure, sentimental dream; but Mrs. Sterne could hardly be expected to understand such fine distinctions, and the letter only strengthened her determination to reach a settlement with her husband.

When Sterne understood the purpose of his wife's visit to him, he tried to persuade her to postpone her return until the following March—"for before that time I should have published my sentimental work and should be in town to receive you—" But he could not deter her, and he resigned himself to her coming. He wrote Lydia that he was lonely, with only his cat for company. "Your lively French dog shall have his place on the other side of my fire;—but if he is as devilish as when I last saw him, I must tutor him; for I will not have my cat abused.—In short, I will have nothing devilish about me:—a combustion will spoil a sentimental thought."

He was still firm about his dislike of the French coquetry in Lydia. "Throw all your *rouge*-pots into the Sorgue before you set out.—I will have no *rouge* put on in England," he wrote, the firm father. But before he had finished the letter, he relented and softened his tone. He urged them to buy whatever they desired in Paris. "Write to me from Paris, that I may come and meet you in my post-chaise, with my long-tailed horses;—and the moment you have both put your feet in it, call it hereafter yours." (So, the carriage which was Eliza's in fancy was to be Mrs. Sterne's in reality. The secret of Sterne's apparent contradictions is thus simply explained.)

To his friends Sterne explained gaily that his wife was coming to fleece him and would leave him stripped bare of all his possessions. Visiting Skelton Castle, where Garrick was a guest, he drew this amusing picture of his domestic troubles—and for contrast he described the charming Eliza, whose picture he passed around among the gentlemen and ladies after supper.

Through the late summer and early autumn Sterne awaited his wife's arrival. His letters to her, by which he hoped to soothe her fears—and perhaps forestall her coming—had gone astray. Mrs. Sterne, quite naturally, interpreted the silence from England as additional proof of her husband's neglect, and fresh fuel was added to the fires of her resentment. It was the middle of September before she was ready to leave the south of France, and on the second day of October she and Lydia arrived in Coxwould.

Sterne met them in York, and drove them in his chaise to the parsonage. Their arrival did not jar him as much as he had anticipated; he was, in fact, happy to see them, and delighted with the improvement in Lydia. Even his wife did not displease him as much as his emotional scribblings in the journal would indicate. Writing to his friends, Mr. and Mrs. James, the day after Mrs. Sterne's arrival, he added a hasty postscript: "My wife and daughter arrived here last night from France.—My girl has returned an elegant, accomplished little slut.—My wife,—but I hate to praise my wife;—'tis as much as decency will

allow, to praise my daughter." Their visit was an amiable
one, lasting two months. It is more than probable that
Sterne would have been glad to forget his charming Bramine and settle down again to a domestic existence with
his wife and Lydia. He made this suggestion to Mrs.
Sterne, but she declared that her health would suffer in
England. It was decided that she and Lydia would take
a house in York for the winter, and return to France in
the spring, to live there permanently. Sterne agreed to
allow her three hundred pounds a year; in addition, he
agreed to turn part of his estate into cash, with which to
purchase an annuity in France of two thousand pounds for
Lydia. All of this he detailed in his final entry in the
journal, dated—erroneously, it should be noted—November 1. The date should have been December 1. Having
concluded with his wife, Sterne added these final words
to Eliza:

—And now Eliza! Let me talk to thee—But what can
I say, What can I write—But the yearnings of a heart
wasted with looking and wishing for thy Return—
Return—Return! my dear Eliza! May heaven smooth
the Way for thee and send thee safely to us, and Joy
for Ever.

The entry has a finality of tone, as though it were an
editorial conclusion to the record of a past emotion. And
such indeed it was, by December 1.

It was a touching scene as Sterne parted from his wife
and daughter. The carriage was ready, waiting outside
the gates of the parsonage. The baggage was packed for
York, and Mrs. Sterne was already seated in the chaise.
Sterne bade Lydia adieu, and pressed into her hand a ten-
pound note. Lydia refused it. "No, my dear papa, our
expenses of coming from France may have straitened you;
—I would rather put an hundred guineas into your pocket

than take ten out of it," she said. Telling the story to his
friend Lee later, Sterne said, "You will laugh at my weak-
ness,—but I cannot help it. . . . I burst into tears."

With Mrs. Sterne and Lydia settled for the winter in
York, Sterne turned back to the writing of his *Sentimental
Journey,* interrupted by their visit. Throughout the last
weeks of his London season, he had been busy gathering
subscriptions for the first installment. He had made elaborate plans for its publication, and hoped to make it a
large quarto volume. As it finally appeared, however, the
installment was published in two small volumes. Again
Sterne had been successful in securing a brilliant patronage for his work, although the list was not half so long
as that which had ushered his sermons into the world.

As has already been noted, the *Sentimental Journey* was
written under the influence of Sterne's fantastic love for
Eliza Draper. It can not be taken as a true account of his
travels or of his attitudes and impressions in France. It
is only a record of his emotional state during the summer
and autumn when he wrote it. Many of the passages are
exquisite, representing the fruition of Sterne's impressionistic—or sentimental—art. It is only necessary to compare
the *Sentimental Journey* with the seventh volume of
Shandy—covering much of the same material—to see the
change which his emotional fancies had wrought in Sterne's
art. The satire there had been altered to sentiment; the
indecencies of *Shandy* are largely absent from Sterne's last
work.

In the last few months of his life, Sterne magnified the
indecencies of *Tristram Shandy.* Through the purifying
influence of an unreal passion and a too-real disease, he
began to believe he had done wrong in catering to the
public taste for obscenity. The *Sentimental Journey* was to
be in part an offering to the outraged gods of decency; by it

Sterne hoped to purge his soul, appease his enemies and cleanse his reputation. While he was at work on it, he wrote the Jameses, "I told you my design in it was to teach us to love the world and our fellow-creatures better than we do:—so it runs most upon those gentler passions and affections, which aid so much in it." To another friend he wrote, "If it is not thought a chaste book, mercy on them that read it, for they must have warm imaginations indeed!"

Sterne was thorough and painstaking in this work. Professor Cross devotes much attention to the revisions in the original manuscript. Many of the passages which might have given offense were altered and cleansed. Awkward phrases were revised for happier ones, and some of these phrases have become by-words of the language. How many clergymen, looking in vain through the Old and New Testaments for the source of the phrase, "God tempers the wind to the shorn lamb," would be shocked to learn that it comes from the *verboten* works of Sterne?

Sterne planned to have the volumes ready by Christmas, and he promised his friends that he would be in town for the holiday season. But before we leave Coxwould for the last time with the errant parson, there are two matters worth our attention. The first concerns Sterne's status in the church in the last year of his life. Offers of preferment showered in upon him; the church was as anxious as the worldly laymen to honor the most famous man of letters in England. The Bishop of Cork and Ross, whom Sterne met at Scarborough, offered him high preferment if he would settle in Ireland. Another offer came from a friend in the south, who wanted Sterne to exchange the livings of Sutton and Stillington for Surry, only thirty miles from London, and worth three hundred and fifty pounds a year. With this, Sterne could retain the living

of Coxwould. These were flattering offers, which Sterne
would have grasped eagerly a few years before. But now
he was ill, worn out with the consumption that was fast
wasting his life. He had, also, tired of the church; the
fire of the preacher, never strong in him, had receded to
a low ebb.

Another incident, not important but amusing, shows
the Shandaic strain still strong in the man. In October,
he received a letter from an unidentified admirer in London, known to us only as Hannah. Whether he could not
recollect his meeting with her, or only pretended to have
forgotten her, we can not be sure, but his answer is in
the strain of the old Sterne, and deserves to be quoted:

> Ever since my dear H. wrote me word she was mine
> more than ever woman was, I have been racking my
> memory to inform me where it was that you and I
> had that affair together.—People think that I have
> had many (some in body, some in mind); but as I
> told you before, you have had me more than any
> woman; therefore, you must have had me, H——, both
> in mind and in body.—Now I cannot recollect where
> it was, nor exactly when:—it could not be the Lady
> in Bond-street, or Grosvenor-street, or —— Square, or
> Pall-Mall.—We shall make it out, H——, when we
> meet; I emphatically long for it; 'tis no matter; I
> cannot now stand writing to you today:—I will
> make it up next post,—for dinner is upon the table;
> and if I make Lord F—— stay, he will not frank this.—
> How do you do? Which parts of Tristram do you
> like best?—God bless you.

Evidently Hannah identified herself properly in her next
letter, and by the middle of November Sterne was writing
to her in his most familiar vein:

> Now be a good dear woman, my H——, and execute
> these commissions well;—and when I see you, I will

give you a kiss:—there's for you!—But I have something
else for you, which I am fabricating at a great rate,
and that is my Sentimental Journey, which shall make
you cry as much as it has affected me,—or I will give
up the business of sentimental writing,—and write to
the body;—that is, H——, what I am doing in writing
to you:—but you are a *good body,* which is worth half
a score mean souls.

Toward the end of December, Sterne was ready for the
London visit, and by the first of January he was again
settled in his rooms at 41 Old Bond Street.   He was, as
usual, soon "tied down neck and heels (twice over) by engagements."   The work of seeing his volumes through the
printer's was more difficult this year and required more
of his time.   It became necessary to postpone the appearance of the work several times, and it was not placed on
sale until after the middle of February.

A Sentimental Journey Through France and Italy had
an immediate vogue, and its popularity has continued to
the present day.   Within a year after its publication, it
had been translated into French and German, and was
being widely read throughout Europe.   The critics who
had attacked Sterne most severely softened perceptibly,
and Walpole, who was bored by *Shandy,* praised the *Sentimental Journey* for its "good nature and strokes of delicacy."   Among the general public, the *Sentimental Journey* has long outranked *Tristram Shandy* in popularity.
The reasons are obvious.   It is by no means as difficult to
read, for Sterne did not resort so much to asterisks, typographical oddities or obscure expressions.   The reader
was not asked to follow a bare thread of a story through
long and often pointless digressions.   Finally, because
Sterne did not slash here at the fabric of life, the reader
is not under the obligation of following him through ob-

scure and bitter satires. Sterne the crusader had given way to Sterne the sentimentalist; the realist was vanquished by the artist of delicacy. If *Tristram Shandy* is by far more important, at least *A Sentimental Journey* is more appealing to the casual reader.

Sterne intended to continue the story of his travels, and expected to bring out the concluding two volumes, on Italy, in the following year. But by the time the first installment was published, he was already nearing the end of his turbulent career. He had come to London worn out by his illness, hoping to gain in health by the change from Coxwould's solitude. But in town his health failed rapidly, and on several occasions he was forced to break engagements with his dear friends, the Jameses. We see him through the month of February, going about on his social rounds, despite his illness. He was made happy by a gift from a Dr. Eustace, in America. The gift, a Shandaic walking-stick with two carved handles, Sterne compared to *Shandy*. "—The parallel breaks only in this, that in using the stick, every one will take the handle which suits his convenience. In Tristram Shandy the handle is taken which suits the passions, their ignorance, or their sensibility. There is so little true feeling in the herd of the world, that I wish I could have got an act of parliament, when the books first appeared, that none but wise men should look into them." A friend sent him some prints, which he promised to hang in his study at Coxwould. But even then the shadow of death was ominous, for he added the prophetic words, "—if I recover from my ill state of health—"

Toward the end of February Sterne appeared in public for the last time. On a Sunday, he breakfasted with a friend, fulfilled an engagement with Lord Ossory and in the evening attended a dinner-party at the James house in

Gerard Street. Returning to his rooms, he found himself in a fever, and he was forced to his bed. As word went around the circles Sterne had frequented, that he was ill, his rooms became a center of attention. From morning until evening his friends came in to visit him. Sterne occupied himself writing on a comic "romance" which has never been discovered, and which was probably destroyed immediately after his death.

Despite the seriousness of his condition, he was confident that he would recover. In a letter to Mrs. Montagu he wrote, "I feel my existence strongly, and something like revelation along with it, which tells, I shall not dye—but live—" But the resurgent spirit of Jester Yorick could not forever save him. In the first two weeks of March his illness grew steadily worse, developing from influenza to pleurisy. To Lydia he wrote, "—if I escape, 'twill not be for a long period, my child—unless a quiet retreat and peace of mind can restore me." Lydia was disturbed by a report that Sterne intended—if his daughter were left an orphan—to put her under the guardianship of Eliza. Sterne denied this, indicating that Mrs. James was his choice as his daughter's benefactress.

As his condition grew worse and death seemed imminent, Sterne's thoughts turned more and more to Lydia. By March 15 Sterne was so enfeebled that he could hardly hold a pen, but he managed to write a last letter to Mrs. James:

> My spirits are fled;—'tis a bad omen.—Do not weep, my dear Lady;—your tears are too precious to shed for me;—bottle them up, and may the cork never be drawn!—Dearest, kindest, gentlest, and best of women! may health, peace, and happiness, prove your handmaids!—If I die, cherish the remembrance of me, and forget the follies which you so often condemned,—

which my heart, not my head, betrayed me into.
Should my child, my Lydia, want a mother, may I
hope you will (if she is left parentless) take her to
your bosom?—You are the only woman on earth I can
depend on for such a benevolent action.—I wrote to
her a fortnight ago, and told her what, I trust, she
will find in you.—Mr. J—— will be a father to her;—
he will protect her from every insult; for he wears
a sword which he has served his country with, and
which he would know how to draw out of the scab-
bard in defence of innocence. Commend me to him,
as I now commend you to that Being who takes under
his care the good and kind part of the world.—
Adieu—

Mr. James was often in Sterne's rooms toward the end.
Yet death found Sterne alone. Perhaps in those last hours,
Sterne thought of the wish he had written in jest:

> Was I in a condition to stipulate with Death, as I am
> this moment with my apothecary, how and where I
> will take his clyster—I should certainly declare against
> submitting to it before my friends; and therefore I
> never seriously think upon the mode and manner of
> this great catastrophe . . . . but I constantly draw the
> curtain across it with this wish . . . . that it happen
> not to me in my own house—but rather at some de-
> cent inn—at home, I know it—the concern of my
> friends, and the last services of wiping my brows, and
> soothing my pillow, which the quivering hand of
> pale affection shall pay me, will so crucify my soul,
> that I shall die of a distemper which my physician is
> not aware of: but in an inn, the few cold offices I
> wanted, would be purchased with a few guineas, and
> paid me with an undisturbed, but punctual atten-
> tion——

How calmly prophetic the words must have seemed that
Friday, the eighteenth of March, 1768. Just a short distance from Sterne's apartment, "Fish" Crawford, his friend,

was entertaining a group of men, among them Garrick and Mr. James. The conversation turned to Sterne, and Crawford sent out John Macdonald, who was in his service, to find out whether there had been a change in Sterne's condition.

Macdonald went to Sterne's lodgings and asked the landlady about her famous tenant. She told him to go up to Sterne's rooms. Sterne was alone, except for the nurse and a servant-girl. Macdonald stood by the door for a few minutes. He saw Sterne raise his hand, "as if to stop a blow," and he heard the faint words, "Now it is come," as death met face to face a man so long pursued.

affected by the news of his death. One of his friends said

XIX

Shandean Conclusion

Lᴏɴᴅᴏɴ and all of Europe received with varying reactions the news of Yorick's death. When John Macdonald
returned to his master to tell him of Sterne's passing,
he reported "the gentlemen were all very sorry, and lamented him very much." The newspapers printed brief
stories of his death, some of them quoting philosophically
the famous lines of Hamlet over the grave of Yorick: "Alas,
poor Yorick! I knew him, Horatio: a fellow of infinite
jest, of most excellent fancy. . . . Where be your gibes
now? Your gambols? Your songs? Your flashes of merri-
ment that were wont to set the table on a roar? Not one
now, to mock your own grinning?" It was said that "he
died as he lived . . . not in the least affected by the prospect of his approaching dissolution." Within a week or
two after Sterne's death, scribblers were writing sardonic
pieces for the magazines: one of them wondered whether
Yorick had ascended to Elysian fields or had gone down to
the regions of Pluto. Other magazines, notably the *London Magazine*, which had championed Sterne's work during his lifetime, came to his defense, drawing a pretty
moral from Sterne's own lines: "—The Accusing Spirit,
which flew up to heaven's chancery with the oath, blushed
as he gave it in;—and the Recording Angel, as he wrote

it down, dropped a tear upon the word, and blotted it out for ever."

Those who had known Sterne intimately were deeply affected by the news of his death. One of his friends said sadly that Sterne had taken his last "sentimental journey." In France and Germany, where Sterne had already been widely read and admired, the report of Sterne's death shocked many of his literary contemporaries. It is said that Lessing exclaimed, "I would have given ten years of my own life, if I had been able to lengthen Sterne's by one."

The members of Sterne's family and his Yorkshire friends were all away from London at the time of his death. Arrangements for the funeral were probably made by Becket, the publisher, and Mr. James. Sterne's body was buried in the grounds belonging to St. George's Church, in Hanover Square. According to tradition only two mourners accompanied the coach to the burial grounds, and if this is true, the two men were probably Becket and James. How many of Sterne's famous friends came to pay their last respects before the burial we can not know, but it seems reasonable to suppose there were many.

Shortly after Sterne's interment, London began to hear a strange story. It was whispered that Sterne's grave had been opened by grave-robbers, who had taken his body to Cambridge and sold it there for dissection. The professor of anatomy invited two friends in to see the dissection, and one of them, when the operation was nearly completed, uncovered the face and recognized Sterne. This was the story, and it has persisted through more than a century and a half. If it is true, the moralists can point to the fitness of this gruesome end for an errant jester! Numerous attempts have been made to trace the story. Examinations have been made of the skulls in the Cambridge collection,

but amid the welter of rumors and denials, it is impossible
to learn the truth.   This much is certain—the practice of
disinterring bodies from unmarked graves to be sold for
dissection was common at the time.   Because of the dis-
repute in which the work was held, anatomists were forced
to stoop to this traffic to secure subjects for experiment.
The burial-ground which held Sterne's last remains was
far out of the line of travel, in the suburbs of the city, and
ghouls operated there with a great degree of impunity,
although efforts had been made to halt them.   If Sterne's
body did come to this end, it would never have been publicly admitted, out of fear of adverse public opinion.   So
we can only conjecture—as all London did—over the story.

Sterne's friends considered erecting a stone to his memory, and Garrick wrote an epitaph:

> Shall Pride a heap of sculptur'd marble raise,
> Some worthless, unmourn'd titled fool to praise;
> And shall we not by one poor grave-stone learn
> Where Genius, Wit, and Humour, sleep with Sterne?

However, because of the belief that Sterne's body was no
longer in the burial-ground, Garrick gave up his plan, and
Sterne's grave remained unmarked for twenty years.   At
that time, two Freemasons, seeing in Sterne—strangely
enough—a brother spirit, erected a headstone, engraved
with a design, a long eulogy in verse, and the commonplace
lament, "Alas!   Poor Yorick."   His age and date of birth
were erroneous as given on this stone, and the "brother
masons," not content with their long poem of praise, added
the following explanation: "This monumental Stone was
erected to the memory of the deceased, by two Brother
Masons: for although he did not live to be a member of
their Society, yet all his incomparable Performances evidently prove him to have acted by Rule and Square: they

rejoice in this opportunity of perpetuating his high and irreproachable character to after ages." We can imagine Sterne, grinning the satyr-like grin of Reynolds' portrait —in Elysian fields or in the hold of Pluto! During the last century a more fitting foot stone was erected, and a bronze tablet near the gate of the Coxwould parsonage serves to remind the visitor of the genius that was Sterne's.

Sterne left no will. Shortly after his death, a relative of Mrs. Sterne went to the rooms in Old Bond Street and took charge of Sterne's personal effects and papers. Many of the latter he destroyed, including probably the romance on which Sterne had been working the week before his death. It is unfortunate that the selection of "loose papers" to be destroyed was placed by circumstances in the hands of such a careless editor. With a fire conveniently near, he burned whatever he did not consider worth keeping. Sterne's affairs, at his death, were hardly in perfect order, but they were not as bad as tradition has it. In April his books, horses and household goods were sold, bringing four hundred pounds.

Creditors began immediately to send in their bills. When Mrs. Sterne totalled these, she found a debt of 1,100 pounds to be settled. However, this included funeral expenses and the loss of the parsonage at Sutton, burnt down by the carelessness of the curate, estimated at some three hundred pounds. When these items are subtracted, it will be seen that Sterne's personal debts are not too wildly extravagant. Out of a feeling of honor, Mrs. Sterne undertook to pay all these debts from the income of her properties, amounting to some fifty pounds a year. This was a pretty gesture, but little more, for she could not possibly have accomplished this.

All of Sterne's debts were eventually paid. Mrs. Sterne and Lydia were aided by a collection of eight hundred pounds, taken up by Hall-Stevenson and others of Sterne's friends, at the York races in the summer. Another hundred pounds came from Sterne's intimate friends in London. Mrs. Sterne, however, refused to rebuild the parsonage at Sutton, claiming, and rightly so, that the damage had been caused through no fault of Sterne's, and that the parsonage had been practically worthless before Sterne had rebuilt it in 1741 at his own expense. The current incumbent brought suit against the estate, which was finally compromised upon payment of sixty pounds.

Among Sterne's papers were found a letter book, in which he had made copies of many of his letters, anticipating their publication after his death, and some eighteen sermons, which he had left over after culling the best for his four volumes. The sermons were brought to London by Mrs. Sterne and Lydia in the spring of 1769, and were published in June in three small volumes. The publication was financed by a combine of publishers, one of whom was Becket. If we can interpret correctly Lydia's correspondence regarding the volumes, they brought about four hundred pounds for the copyright and the mother and daughter received the proceeds of the subscriptions which they solicited.

It had been as well for Sterne's reputation had these sermons never been published. Though they are not entirely without merit, still they do not represent Sterne at his best, and the parson had wisely kept them hidden away in his study. Furthermore, Sterne borrowed more liberally from the works of others in writing these sermons than in anything else he wrote. Many of the charges of plagiarism find support in the three volumes, although it is clear that Sterne's intention was not to claim for himself the credit of another's work. These sermons were written hastily, in the course of his parish duties, and when he found it convenient to borrow from other clergymen, he did so. Many of the sermons contain notations on the source of the borrowed material.

While Mrs. Sterne and Lydia were in London, Hall-Stevenson appeared on the scene with the manuscript of the concluding two volumes of the *Sentimental Journey*. These were published as a continuation of Sterne's travels by his friend Eugenius, prepared from Sterne's notes. As a matter of fact, Hall-Stevenson merely rewrote the first two volumes, depicting Sterne as revisiting the scenes there described.

Numerous other projects were set on foot to turn Sterne's reputation to profit. Lydia suggested that Hall-Stevenson and Wilkes collaborate on a biography of her father. Along with this was to be published a new complete edition of *Tristram Shandy*, for which Lydia would prepare the drawings. After a long and unsatisfactory correspondence, the project fell through. Lydia and her mother retired to France, settling at Angoulême.

The next year at Angoulême was a troubled one. The project for the biography fell through, and mother and daughter were left almost destitute. They could never manage to live within their means, and were always in desperate need. At this point Eliza Draper, the Bramine of Sterne's last months, came again into the affairs of the Sterne family. News had somehow come to her in India that her name was to be linked publicly with Sterne's through the publication of their correspondence. Eliza foresaw clearly that the public would not interpret these letters in a wholesome spirit, and she was horrified at the rumor. Knowing only one way to halt their publication, she offered money to Mrs. Sterne and Lydia, and agreed also to reimburse Becket for any loss he might suffer by withholding the letters. A prettier name might be given the transaction, but to speak plainly, it was blackmail; and through this blackmail Lydia and Mrs. Sterne received from Eliza an amount variously estimated at more than a hundred pounds.

In 1772, Lydia married Jean Baptiste Alexandre de Medalle. The marriage took place in spite of Mrs. Montagu's advice; in a letter to Lydia, the Bluestocking leader warned her of the difference in religion and the fact that such a marriage would leave Mrs. Sterne almost destitute. But Lydia was without choice in the matter, if we interpret literally an entry in the register at Albi, where the marriage vows were said. The marriage, according to this entry, was urgent, *"car alors la loi autorisait la recherche de la paternité."* Fitzgerald interprets this generously to mean that the marriage was necessary immediately because of Mrs. Sterne's illness and the possibility of her death. However, it is difficult to be so generous, and it is pretty generally agreed that Lydia was *enceinte* before her marriage.

The marriage took place in April, 1772. By that time Mrs. Sterne's illness was indeed serious. Her early mental condition had again returned, and she was subject to epileptic fits. Her death came in January, 1773, only eight months after Lydia's marriage.

Lydia survived her mother by only a few years. Soon after her marriage, a son was born, who was christened in the Catholic faith, which Lydia had adopted. The Medalles disposed of Sterne's Yorkshire properties and settled down in France. However, Lydia's husband, who was five years younger than she, died in 1774, and Lydia returned to England to wrest more money out of her father's papers.

Between 1769 and 1775 many volumes of letters and fragments purporting to be Sterne's had been published in England. With the exception of a volume containing ten letters from Sterne to Eliza, these were largely forgeries. Upon Lydia's return to England in 1775, she found the public eager for anything pertaining to Sterne. She spent several months arranging and editing her collection of letters, more than one hundred in all, and in October, 1775, these were published in three volumes. In addition to the letters, the volumes contained the autobiographical fragment quoted in the first chapters of this work, *An Impromptu,* and a *Fragment in the Manner of Rabelais.* The edition was illustrated with an engraving of Lydia leaning over a bust of her father.

It would take an entire chapter to describe adequately the extent to which Lydia's editing emasculated Sterne's letters. In general, her method was to eliminate all disrespectful or jocund references to her mother, substitute her own name for Eliza's in several passages, change the wording wherever it pleased her fancy, and turn the phrases against Eliza wherever possible. Many of the letters she dated erroneously. However, the volumes remain the most extensive source of information about Sterne, and she did the world a service in giving it Sterne's delightful little autobiography.

The rest of Lydia's life remains uncertain. With her work in England successfully completed, she went back to France, where she died within the next few years. Her son died at the age of ten, ending the direct line of descent from Sterne.

Sterne's Bramine survived him by only a few years, also. Upon her return to India in 1767, she took up again her "unbearable" life with her husband. After some reverses in Draper's fortune, husband and wife began a series of bitter quarrels, which came to a climax in January, 1773. Each accused the other of inconstancy, and Eliza eloped with one of her numerous admirers. For a time she lived under the protection of her uncle in Masulipatam. However, she quarreled with him, very likely over her flirtations, and in 1774 she returned to England.

In England she found herself the center of much attention and curiosity. The volume containing the ten letters from Sterne to Eliza had been published and was being read with avidity. Eliza's return to England increased the demand, and several editions were brought out. Several forgeries also appeared, as might be expected, and among these was a volume of letters purportedly written by Eliza to Sterne. For many years these letters were accepted as genuine.

Her affairs with Wilkes, Combe, and the Abbé Raynal have already been commented on. After a short notoriety in the limelight, Eliza disappeared from the public view, and on August 3, 1778, she died. She lies buried in the cathedral at Bristol, where her life is commemorated by a beautiful monument.

XX

Sterne: An Impression

WHAT was Sterne? Ferriar made him a plagiarist, Byron a hypocrite, Thackeray a scoundrel. In these latter days, after psychoanalysis became the vogue, he has been called a sexual frustrate. In short, there is no calumny against man or writer which Sterne's frail shoulders have not been called upon to carry in the century and a half since his death. And even those who have occasionally risen in his behalf have damned him with faint praise, either through lack of understanding or fear of seeming to approve what it has long been conventional to disapprove. "It is impossible," wrote a recent critic, "not to love the creator of Uncle Toby; impossible to respect Laurence Sterne." This naive assertion represents so completely the crux of conventional thought on Sterne that it may well serve to introduce these concluding pages.

What was Sterne, the man? Shaped in the mold of adversity, he developed a philosophy of life that the intelligent mind can not help but admire. His keen delight in living enabled him to overcome adversities which would have tried to the limit men with stronger constitutions. All his life he fought against the twin demons of disease and poverty, and out of this long struggle came a hedonism which could meet every new day with new hope—which could bring a measure of contentment into any situation. "We must bring three parts in four of the treat along with us," he wrote several years before his death. "In short, we must be happy within, and then few things without us make much difference. This is my Shandean philosophy." When death knocked on his door, he turned it away with a jest, and when at last its shadow hovered over his bed, he met it with calm resignation.

Sterne's was a full life, lived with zest. He loved good living, good books, and beautiful women. He delighted in the companionship of intelligent men, and he could feel a thrill at the swift motion of horses on the course at York. It is significant that he numbered among his most intimate friends the greatest wits of his age, as well as its truest gentlemen. It must remain a lasting tribute to Sterne that he could hold the friendship of such men as David Garrick, Commodore James, Lord Bathurst, and the young Sir James Macdonald. His death was mourned, not only as the passing of a genius, but a gentleman as well. Contrary to tradition, the drawing rooms that had echoed the mirth of Sterne's jests felt a loss at his passing.

As a man of the church, Sterne fulfilled his duties beyond the slightest reproach. His entry into the church was more a matter of circumstance than choice, for he never felt himself inspired with the zeal of the preacher. Sterne was too intelligent to become the sort of partisan that the vocation of the preacher demands. He was too clearly aware of the blunders and hypocrisies of organized religion, and he could not bring himself to participate in the childish intrigues of the church circles. Nevertheless, Sterne felt his duty here, as everywhere, and to the last he was conscientious in the performance of his work.

In considering Sterne as a clergyman, we must consider the standards of his age. The clergy of his time was allowed a greater degree of freedom than at any time since. Men of the cloth could engage in the ordinary activities of other gentlemen without bringing upon themselves the censure of the church or the laity. Thus Sterne could attend with impunity the races, the fashionable entertainments of London, and the gatherings of his convivial friends. His affairs of the heart could become a matter for public discussion, with little danger of censure and no danger of unfrocking.

This matter of Sterne's love affairs has been too often urged as sufficient reason for his damnation. In this, our age defers to the Victorian, for the whole argument can be traced back to a group of Victorian critics, notably Thackeray. The fact is, that Sterne's own age, and his intimate friends, especially, found little to censure in his conduct. He had been unfortunate in his marriage, and while he remained in many respects a dutiful husband, it is too much to expect that he should have pretended a love for a nagging shrew of a wife long after that love had ceased to exist. Sterne was one of those men—and there are many—who are constitutionally unsuited to marriage. He was a man of individual character who writhed under any sort of domination. His temperament he could not blend with another, especially when that other was a temperament of the type of Elizabeth Lumley. She could not understand the philosophy by which Sterne threw himself gaily into mad projects; her stolidity could not comprehend his want of discretion; her humorless mind could not appreciate his genius. They drifted rapidly apart, and by the time Sterne began to seek out his various Dulcineas, Elizabeth Lumley had become indifferent to the love he no longer offered. Sterne's loves, harmless as they proved to be, were a soothing balm without which his philosophy of life would have been incomplete.

Out of the adversities of his early life came the genius
of Sterne's last years.   But for the quarrels and recriminations in York, the world might never have had *Tristram
Shandy*.   Into this work, which has kept Sterne's fame
alive through more than a century and a half, Parson
Yorick poured the bitterness and wisdom of a lifetime.
If his work was unpopular with prudes and moralists, it
was because Sterne spoke of the follies and foibles of his
age with a too-distinct clarity.   His denunciations, couched
as they were in the phrases of humor and indelicacy, were
nevertheless apparent.   It is unfortunate that a part, at
least, of Sterne's present fame rests on a misinterpretation.
"It is impossible," writes the conventional commentator,
"not to love the creator of Uncle Toby."   Thus my uncle
Toby, through whom Sterne fabricated his cleverest and
most heart-felt satire, has become a symbol of naive virtue
and prudish morality.   If Sterne's bones still rest in a
grave in suburban London, how they must writhe.

Out of the pleasant memories of his boyhood in the
barracks, his biographers believed, came the character of
my uncle Toby and the battlegrounds on the bowling-
green.   How the sensitive boy must have hated the army
life which made his existence a hardship.   What terror he
must have felt as he saw his tiny brothers and sisters fall
victims, one by one, to the nomadic existence of the camp
followers.   And if there remained a final impression to
seal his hatred of the military life, it must have come with
the death of his father, whom he loved.   That "little smart
man" at last fell as a sacrifice to the gods of war.   And out
of this hatred came the battlegrounds on the bowling-
green, and the naive figure of my uncle Toby and Trim.
Who can believe that the naïveté and complete lack of
sophistication of my uncle Toby really represented Sterne's
ideal of humanity?   In more than one place Sterne dropped

the military satire in my uncle Toby and allowed his bitterness to surge forth.

Sterne's primary urge to write came from no motive
baser than his desire to express his feelings and attitudes.
In a world of folly, his would be the one clear voice of
denunciation. It is not to Sterne's discredit that he chose
to express himself as he did—sometimes indelicately. What
he had to say was not for those who would pale at a harsh
word, or for those whose minds could be corrupted by a
phrase. However, finding a popular market for indelicacy, he succumbed for a time to the lure of fame and
money, and fabricated grossnesses for their own sake. It
would be hard to forgive Sterne this transgression, had
he not grown tired himself of this falseness to his purpose
and altered his ways. In the later installments of *Tristram*
it was again the honest Sterne who wrote. The indelica-
cies were still there, but now Sterne remembered again
his purpose in writing, and rewove into his work the fabric by which he hoped to attain immortality. In the last
installment Sterne confidently predicted that posterity
should thumb the pages of his books. "—I say, by Posterity
—and care not, if I repeat the word again—for what has
this book done more than the Legation of Moses, or the
Tale of a Tub, that it may not swim down the gutter of
Time along with them?"

Where, in all of this, is Sterne the sentimentalist? Although he proclaimed himself a sentimentalist, he was
hardly that, in our current sense of the word. His maudlin tears were not the dominant characteristic of the man,
but merely a minor facet of a broad surface. Sterne was
a man of feeling, an impressionist. His writings were as
personal as the shape of a well-worn pair of shoes, as personal as a vagary before an open fireplace, or an intimate
conversation; and even today, when many of the allusions

are lost and much of the satire become a truism, the man
is to be found in his pages, recorded as a living and lively
being. He scorned the impersonal formalities of conventional narrative, and thus laid the foundations for a school
of literature now dominant throughout the world. Volumes have been written, and volumes may still be written, on Sterne's influence on the literature of feeling—in
England, on the Continent, and wherever his writings have
penetrated. Nearly every civilized language has its trans-
lations of Sterne's books.

Much has been said about Sterne's so-called "plagiarisms." Some half a century after Sterne's death, a Dr.
Ferriar traced the sources of Sterne's material, and published his findings in a volume called *Illustrations of
Sterne*. Among the authors from whom Sterne "borrowed"
he included Burton, Rabelais, Beroalde de Verville, Bou-
chet, Scarron, Swift, Bacon, and Montaigne. Ferriar's "illustrations" are too damning to be entirely overlooked;
there can be no doubt that Sterne was indebted, not only
for ideas, but for whole sentences and paragraphs, to the
authors listed. Yet a careful study of the examples indicates that Sterne has little for which to stand at the bar
of judgment. Many of the sentences he took from Burton
were merely paraphrases of others' writings. In many instances Sterne improved upon his "borrowed" materials.
Occasionally he was able to turn a phrase ironically, and
in almost every instance the material took on a vastly
greater aspect under Sterne's ministrations than in the
original. We have forgiven Shakespeare his borrowed
plots, for they emerged from his pen vastly superior; daily
we forgive musical composers who borrow phrases or
themes. Time and critical judgment have vindicated
Sterne.

Although Sterne had little zeal for the institution of

religion, he was, in part at least, a reformer. In another age, he might have become a champion of peace and human equality. Even in his own age, his was a voice for the future. He foresaw a period of universal tolerance, when all men could live as free men, and black would be equal to white. The voice that denounced hypocrisy and bigotry spoke in horror of the Inquisition, and pleaded gently for human understanding.

The world of books owes much to Laurence Sterne. We shall not overpay him by granting the little charity he asked at the end: "—cherish the remembrance of me, and forget the follies which you so often condemned,—which my heart, not my head betrayed me into—"

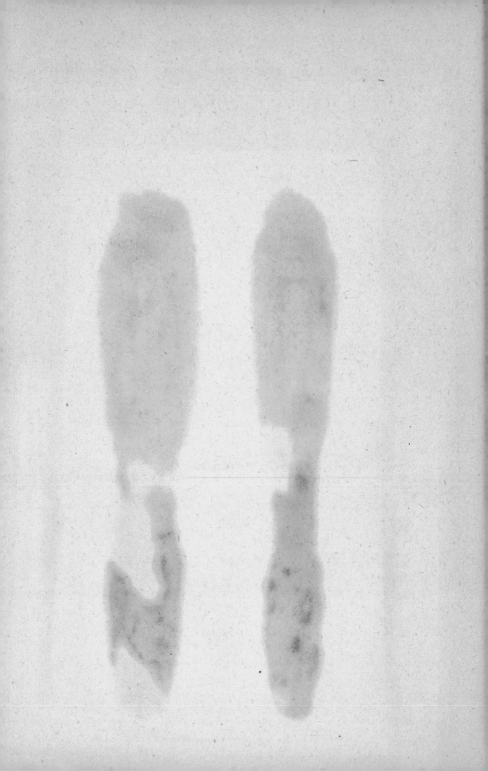

DATE DUE
